£3.50

LANCASHIRE'S GHOSTS AND LEGENDS

Lancashire's Ghosts and Legends

Terence W. Whitaker

ROBERT HALE · LONDON

Robert Hale Limited
Clerkenwell House
Clerkenwell Green
London EC1R 0HT

Photoset by Specialised Offset Services Limited, Liverpool
and printed in Great Britain by
Lowe & Brydone Printers Ltd.,
Thetford, Norfolk.

CONTENTS

For Marjorie and Julia
With Love

ILLUSTRATIONS

All photographs are by the author, except 'Todd
Cottage, Melling' which was taken by John Mulroy.

PREFACE

Ask the average person if he believes in ghosts, and he will more often than not deny their existence yet, at the same time will admit to being a little afraid of the supernatural. Even people who say they have heard or seen 'something' for which there does not appear to be a rational explanation, will continue to be sceptical about ghosts. But, in the consideration of the evidence I have gathered over the years, coupled with my own experiences, it would seem that either a large number of people have been victims of some kind of delusion, or ghosts really do exist.

Ghosts have been recorded as far back as the second century BC. The Greek philosopher Athenodus carried out what must have been the first recorded case of psychical research in the first century BC, and research has been carried out right up until the present day.

The term 'ghost' describes a wide variety of apparitions and paranormal phenomena, but the Lancashire ghosts can be conveniently divided into two major groups: traditional and legendary phantoms, such as those of monks, grieving lovers, grey ladies or victims of some dastardly deed committed during the more violent period of our history, which we have all heard about but only a few can claim to have seen; and the more ordinary phantoms which have been seen by numerous folk, drunk or sober, whose appearance cannot be explained.

In a lot of cases the reasons behind the most persistent hauntings have long been forgotten. Numerous anonymous white ladies walk the corridors of their old homes, seemingly quite oblivious of any living witness or of the effect they might have on them. It may be that such apparitions are the result of emotions so intense that, in some way we do not yet understand, they have left some kind of visible imprint in the atmosphere which a few people are sensitive enough to intercept in some way and see as phantoms. This could explain why one person in a group may be suddenly terrified by something, while the remainder may be totally unaware of anything wrong. Not all apparitions are in a human form either: others include animals, phantom coaches, motor-cars, ships, funeral hearses and even aircraft.

It has been said that Britain is the country of ghosts, the most haunted country in Europe. Personally I do not think it is any more haunted than the rest of Europe, but now that we have lost our Empire, the only thing we have left to hang on to are our traditions; therefore we probably cherish our ghosts more. Indeed, there is not a country house between Land's End and John o'Groats that does not have either a screaming skull or a resident phantom.

In many respects, the ghosts and legends of Britain tell much about the history of the country, and certainly the turbulent and often violent history of Lancashire is reflected in many of the stories and legends in this book. Many of the older ghost traditions are accounted for by folk memory – the story of an event handed down from one generation to the next, satisfying man's need for stories and becoming distorted in the re-telling but retaining through the centuries a grain of fact.

The first part of this book consists mainly of the personal experiences of people I have met or who have written to tell me of the ghosts and apparitions in their homes. Many are still haunted but have learned to live with (and, in at least one case, have become fond of) their uninvited guests. A number of the stories contained within these pages have never been in print before; others are having another airing. I have not set out with the deliberate intention of terrifying my readers, nor have I tried to answer many of the questions surrounding these ghosts and poltergeists. In the main I have recorded the paranormal experiences as they were presented to me by numerous honest and intelligent Lancastrians.

The second part tells of historical ghosts and legends – tales which have been related around countless firesides for centuries and which, even in these days of technological advancement, have lost none of their appeal. These stories are as much a part of Lancashire's heritage as are clogs and black puddings, and it would be a tragedy if they were to be forgotten in this enlightened age.

Many people of diverse ways of life have helped me to write this book. To these people I owe a great debt and offer my sincere thanks for their assistance, for the many kindnesses shown to me and for the time they have taken to explain to me, in some detail, their often complicated stories. My thanks also to Ewen Pidgeon for the illustrations and cover design, and to my wife Marjorie and daughter Julia for their help, encouragement and patience and for following me around many haunted sites, where lesser mortals would tremble.

There are some people who deserve a special mention: the editors of the *Burnley Express, Lancaster Guardian, Clitheroe Advertiser, Bolton Evening News, Lancashire Life, Blackpool Gazette and Herald, Southport Visitor, West Lancashire Evening Gazette* and *North-East Lancashire Newspapers*, for kindly inserting my letters asking for any information about hauntings etc; Mike Marsh and BBC Radio Blackburn, for allowing me time on their 'Grapevine' programme; the librarians and their staff, in particular the staff at Burnley Central Library and St Helens Central Library, who went to some considerable trouble to furnish me with information; the staff at Whalley Abbey, Chingle Hall, Samlesbury Hall, Towneley Hall, Hall-i' th'Wood, Smithills Hall and Rufford Old Hall, for their patience in answering my numerous questions, and the following people, who told me of their experiences and kindly gave me permission to mention their names: Mr and Mrs C. Bowker, Kirkby Lonsdale; Mrs J. Elder, late of the Barry Elder Doll Museum, Croston; Mr and Mrs M.L. Fowler, Preston; Mr I.A. Green, manager, Whalley Abbey; Mr R. Hart, St Helens Libraries; Mr A.E. Howarth, Bispham, Blackpool; Mr and Mrs C. Howarth, Rosegrove, Burnley; Mr K. Howarth, Bury Museum; Mrs M. Howarth, Chingle Hall, Goosnargh; Mr C. Howarth (Bill o'Bows), Morecambe; Mrs A. Jessop, Otumoetai, New Zealand; Mrs S. Lord, Burnley; Mrs A. McDougall, Read, Burnley; Mrs D. Millington, Nether Kellett, Carnforth; Mr and Mrs J. Mulroy, Melling, Carnforth; Mrs Nicholls, Grange Park, Blackpool; Mrs E.M. Redmayne, Loughborough; Mrs F. Reynolds, Boothstown, Manchester; Mr K. Senior, director, St Helens Libraries; Mrs M. Smith, Burnley; Mr W.H. Stables, Milnthorpe; Mr and Mrs A. Stephens, Haslingden; Mrs M. Storey, Carnforth; and Mrs J. Whitehead, Silverdale.

Without the help of these lovely people, this book could not have been written, and it is to these people that I humbly dedicate it.

Burnley 1979.

PART ONE
Some Personal Stories

"It is all very well for you who have never seen a ghost
to talk as you do, but had you seen what I witnessed, you
would hold a different opinion!"

Thackeray

1

MESSAGES

There are some people who seem to possess what is commonly known as 'extra-sensory perception'. They just know that something is going to happen, or they have a feeling that something has in fact taken place.

On the other hand, there are events which, if not foretold, are indicated by the presence of some departed relative. I am quite convinced that the ghost of a dead person can materialize to show that some misfortune is imminent. Such has been the experience of Mrs Freda Reynolds, who owns a small grocer's shop in the Boothstown district of Manchester.

Although she herself has never seen the ghost in her shop, she knows it is that of her great-grandmother and that the apparition has been seen by her customers. She told me, "I have not actually seen anything in my shop, but a customer, a very down-to-earth man, heard a woman's voice and saw a hand at the door of my stockroom." The only occupant of the stockroom at that time was her mongrel dog, who was howling. When she went to investigate, Mrs Reynolds found the poor dog shivering with fright, his fur standing on end, nose held high as if pointing towards something at the door. "I don't mind admitting," she said, "this really frightened me."

On another occasion, the door of the stockroom slammed shut just before she was able to get through into the shop, and a force seemed to be holding it, even though she pulled hard, in order to open it again. It is the type of door where the hinges hold it flat against the wall, and there was no draught which could have blown the door shut – indeed, even with the shop door and the back door wide open to create a through flow of air, experiment showed that the door would not blow shut.

Again, this experience frightened her, so much so that she

mentioned it to the next customer who came into the shop.

Now, unknown to Mrs Reynolds, by coincidence this customer was a medium. The customer explained that she had always experienced a strong 'feeling' whenever she came into the shop and said she had actually seen an old lady standing at the stockroom door on a previous occasion, dressed in a black frock with lace sleeves. The medium went on to explain that the 'lady' was warning Mrs Reynolds of some forthcoming trouble and she must take care. The medium also said that she was not to be afraid but to welcome the 'lady' as she was in fact Mrs Reynold's great-grandmother. From that day on, each time she arrived at the shop in the morning, Mrs Reynolds would say, "Good morning, grandma."

However, she did not forget about the warning. As she was stocking shelves one day, she thought the worst thing that could happen would be for her to fall from the step-ladder, but that was not the case, for on the following day, her mother was taken ill with what at first appeared to be a stroke but turned out to be Bell's Palsy.

The next event really scared her for some time afterwards. Again she was alone, when from the stockroom she heard a strange noise, almost as if the whole wall were about to fall down. All the biscuits fell from the shelf and she could hear the dog howling in the stockroom. Mrs Reynolds, thoroughly frightened, ran out into the street, thinking the old shop was about to fall down.

Fortunately, Mrs Reynolds is an intelligent woman and managed quite soon to calm herself down. She went back into the shop to comfort the poor dog, which was still inside the stockroom, surrounded by everything that should have been on the shelves. For about a week after this event nothing else happened, and then, "I remember opening the shop one morning," Mrs Reynolds said, "and I suddenly felt afraid of walking through into the stockroom." She did not know why but felt sure there was someone on the stairs. (These stairs run up between the shop and the stockroom, as they do in many thousands of small Lancashire shops.) Not for one moment did she think there could be a ghost, in fact she thought it might be a burglar. She was so afraid that she ran quickly through the shop, opening all the doors and putting the lights on as she did so. She was so afraid on this occasion that when the bread roundsman came, she asked him if he would go upstairs and check to see if everything was all right. The bread man was no hero either, for he carried an empty milk bottle with him, to use in self-defence. He found nothing and no one, but he too admitted to feeling a presence of some kind.

Two other events occurred which, although of little significance, were quite frightening at the time. On one occasion, a young mother was standing in the shop waiting to be served. On reaching the counter she asked Mrs Reynolds, "Where did the lady go, who was standing in front of the stockroom?" At that time Mrs Reynolds was the only other person in the shop.

The second event was again the stockroom door slamming shut of its own accord. This time she was convinced that something was going to happen to her mother, but the event heralded her father's being suddenly taken ill.

These incidents have taken place over a period of about two years. The medium insists that there is still a presence in the shop, and Mrs Reynolds herself can still feel it, for, as she says, "At no time have I seen anything, but I always know by some uneasy feeling when something dramatic is about to occur."

Mrs Reynolds is a level-headed, unflappable woman, but she has had to admit that these events certainly caused her to be extremely frightened.

Many people believe that all ghosts have to be feared, but this is not so. I know of a number of people who have been convinced that they have been in touch with the supernatural and have felt only a feeling of sorrow or compassion. Take the following incident which happened to Mrs Dorothy Millington some fifteen or sixteen years ago, for example.

Mrs Millington was visiting her daughter at Worsley, Manchester. The day after her arrival was a warm autumn Sunday, so she and her daughter decided to take the dog and have a quiet drive around the Manchester suburbs. They eventually found themselves driving down Hardy Lane at Chorlton-cum-Hardy. Passing the tennis courts, they finally stopped where the road ended at the side of a small river. At this point, a narrow footbridge crossed the river, and the two ladies decided to leave the car and walk the dog.

They found themselves in open parkland, the kind of place where children play and people walk during the summer months. As it was such a nice day, the whole place was alive with people.

Later, and much to Mrs Millington's surprise, the weather suddenly and inexplicably changed from a lovely autumn afternoon to a damp and foggy evening. "I got a horrid feeling of misery and depression," said Mrs Millington, "but strangely enough, no one around me seemed to be bothered or, as you would expect, to begin to make for home."

To the right of where she stood was what appeared to be a sewage-treatment plant. It was not walled in but was enclosed by sloping buttresses. The dog, having been released from his leash, started to run towards the slope and within seconds came back, shivering and stiff, as if terrified. This lasted for some length of time afterwards, and it was obvious the dog had suffered a terrible fright.

As the dog ran back towards them, Mrs Millington noticed that a child was standing beside the buttress – a small, scrawny child with a pinched face, who looked out of keeping with modern times. He did not appear to be a happy, mischievous boy but had an anxious and miserable face. She thought his dress to be of the 1930s era: school cap and badge, dark gaberdine raincoat and short trousers, rather like a middle-class boy attending some smart school or college, and well-disciplined, as boys were in those days. The boy appeared to be playing idly with a blade of grass. He looked straight at Mrs Millington, and he spoke to her. She told me, "I clearly heard him say, 'That man's name is George Ware.'" It all seemed uncanny, particularly as no one other than Mrs Millington appeared to be aware of the boy's presence.

As quickly as it had changed, the weather returned to normal, the activities going on around as if nothing had happened.

In discussing the phenomenon some fifteen years or more after it had happened, one question stands out above all others: who was the little boy? It would seem logical to assume that something had happened near this spot at sometime in the past, but what? Why should Mrs Millington, a visitor from out of town, have seen this pathetic ghost? Was there another story here which to date has remained unpublished?

It was at this point in my research that I had an incredible stroke of luck, which has enabled me to offer a possible clue to the identity of the boy and the reason behind the appearance of the spectre.

Discreet enquiries in the district revealed that a murder had been committed in the area sometime in the middle of the 1930s. A visit to the local library came up with a few details but nothing much in the way of hard facts. It was a chance conversation with an old resident of the area which brought the tragic story to light.

One Saturday evening sometime in the middle thirties, a black fog blanketed Manchester and the suburbs. As the fog swirled during the later afternoon, so the temperature dropped, until by evening it was freezing too.

A difficult, sullen and sometimes awkward boy of about eleven years of age set out on one of his mysterious outings. He was a scholar of St Bede's School, Whalley Range, the child of a second marriage with two step-brothers from his father's previous marriage. Despite the efforts of his elder step-brothers to be kind to him, the boy remained secretive and resentful and had recently taken to sneaking off at night. Where he went, whom he saw and what he did, no one in the family knew.

On this particular night, despite the terrible weather conditions and despite the pleas of his mother to stay indoors, he set out into the murky darkness. He was known to have caught the tram at Chorlton – the tram-crew told police that they remembered trying to persuade him not to alight at the terminus but to go back to town with them, as, owing to the thick fog, the service was being suspended. The tram-crew remembered his being hostile and impudent, and he had insisted on getting off. They saw him walk off into the fog, but before he disappeared, a young man came out of the gateway of a derelict house as if he was waiting to meet him, and the pair of them walked off in the direction of Hardy Lane. The last glimpse the tram-crew had of them, they were walking into the fog, the older man with his arm over the boy's shoulder. Later that night the distraught parents reported the boy missing to the Manchester police.

Sunday dawned bright and cheery, the fog thinned, and by late morning a weak sun had managed to struggle through. A number of local people turned out for their Sunday morning stroll, with the rosy prospect of returning home to a warm lunch.

Two small boys kicking a ball about lost it in the vicinity of the sewage plant and, in looking for it, came across the body of the boy who had been reported missing the previous night. The throat had been cut with such savageness that the head was almost severed from the body. The case has baffled the police since, and I understand that no one was ever charged with the murder. No murder weapon was found, but the autopsy suggested that the boy's throat may have been cut with an open razor. Only one clue was found, a gent's handkerchief, which was identified by the laundry-mark and an initial in one corner as belonging to one of the boy's elder brothers.

The brother, of course, came under suspicion – the motive: jealousy of the youngster or a desire to hurt the parents, due to resentment of the stepmother. However, this could not be proved. The boy, may in fact, have taken the handkerchief out of the house himself.

The crime was more probably of a homosexual nature but would not of course have been reported as such in the Press of the day. In actual fact, apart from a few paragraphs in the local paper, it never made the headlines and was soon forgotten, although it naturally caused a great deal of unhappiness to the family.

So, was the mysterious George Ware the killer of the boy? There are only two people who can answer that question, the murderer and the victim. Could it be that the victim has tried to answer the question for us?

Throughout my period of research for this book I came across many instances of ghosts of the dying appearing to loved ones as if to say goodbye. According to most accounts, there is nothing wraith-like about these apparitions: they seem to be quite solid and normal and are usually mistaken for the living person. However, there are exceptions to every rule, as in the following incident which concerns the Lancashire writer Clifford Howarth, better known to his readers as 'Bill o'Bows'.

In 1966 Clifford was employed as a porter at the Clarendon Hotel on Morecambe's West End promenade. Working with him, also a porter, was a very down-to-earth chap called Harold. The two men became firm friends until Harold took a pub in Lancaster and became his own master. For a couple of years afterwards the two men never saw much of each other.

In those days, there was always a coal fire burning in each of the bars at the Clarendon, and it was Clifford's job to clean them out each morning ready for lighting at ten-thirty, when the bars opened.

One particular morning, having already laid the fire, he went into the back bar. He knelt down in front of the grate and was about to light the fire when, through his knees, he felt the vibrations of someone walking over the wooden floor. Glancing over his shoulder towards the entrance to the bar, he saw what he could only describe as 'a wraith-like mist', or white mass, floating above the floor. It travelled across the top of the bar and moved to the other end of the room. Then, as he watched open-mouthed, the cloud rose and passed through one of the windows.

As it was mid-morning, the room was flooded with daylight, but there was a distinct coldness, and Clifford quickly got the blower to the fire. As the morning passed, he forgot about his experience for a while, but at lunchtime the receptionist sent for him, saying he was wanted on the telephone. The call came from a member of the staff who, on her day off, was shopping in Lancaster and was telephoning from Harold's pub. She told him that Harold had been rushed into Lancaster Royal Infirmary earlier that morning and had died on the operating-table at about ten-thirty!

"I have often wondered," said Clifford, "if the mist I saw in the bar had any connection with the passing of Harold." Apparently, Harold had always desired to own a high-class hotel and had often said that one day he would be 'mine host' at the Clarendon.

Many people are sceptical about spiritualism, believing it to be impossible for anyone to communicate with the dead. Over the years, many spiritualists have been exposed as frauds, but I believe there are genuine receivers who have been given messages, in a variety of ways, from 'the other side'. The following experience has happened to many people in one form or another over the years.

Mrs Pendlebury, a widow, had a small shop in the suburbs of Manchester. One day she was writing out orders, standing at the counter of her shop, when a customer entered, and the harsh 'ping' of the doorbell caused her to look up sharply and push the paper to one side. Having served the customer, Mrs Pendlebury picked up the paper, intent on finishing her order and was surprised at what she saw written there. The writing was definitely her own, but it was the context of what she had written which surprised her.

Subconsciously, she had written a letter to herself, in which she instructed herself to visit Goose Green Church. If she counted a certain number of graves from the east wall of the church, she would find a grave slightly larger than the rest, which she must arrange to have re-opened. In it, she would find at the head of the grave some family jewels which had been lost for years. She had described some of the pieces of jewellery, which included a ring and a watch.

Having read what she had written, Mrs Pendlebury felt quite

foolish, and though she thought it rather extraordinary, she screwed up the paper and threw it in the waste-box under the counter and very soon forgot all about the incident.

Some weeks later, in her flat above the shop, she was writing a letter to a relative when, to her surprise, she found that, again subconsciously, she had written the same letter as she had thrown away a few weeks previously.

This now began to prey on her mind, and she finally decided to consult a spiritualist, who told her she ought to visit the church and make some enquiries, as someone was obviously trying to make contact with her.

Mrs Pendlebury had a brother who was studying for Holy Orders, so she approached him with her story and told him of the advice of the spiritualist. Like most Bible students, her brother did not believe in spiritualism and would not take her seriously, so she decided to go alone to Goose Green, find the church and make her own enquiries.

On arrival at the church, she found a man whom she thought was either the sexton or grave-digger and explained her unusual story to him. He listened politely and said he would help her find the grave. He was as good as his word and, sure enough, several graves from the east wall, they found a grave larger than the others, with a weathered headstone, the writing on which suggested the resting-place of some long-dead relative. The man told her he would need to get permission to open it up, but if she would care to go back in two to three weeks time, he would see what could be done.

Three weeks later, Mrs Pendlebury went back to Goose Green, only to learn that the man to whom she had spoken had left the district under rather mysterious circumstances.

Even as she made her way to the grave she knew that she would find it had been disturbed, and when permission was finally obtained to re-open it, a small box was found which had in fact been forced open but was now empty.

The story does not end there, however. Some time later, Mrs Pendlebury moved out of her shop and bought a newsagent's business in a different part of Manchester. One day, a smartly dressed stranger walked into the shop, and she recognized him as the man to whom she had told her story at Goose Green Church. On his right hand he wore a ring, and hanging from his waistcoat was a watch, both of which were identical to the ones described in the letter.

As she later said, "Who would believe such a story, even if I had laid complaint against this man?"

So there we have four people, of differing backgrounds, each being given a message of one kind or another by the spirit of a dead person. I do not suppose one can call them ghosts in the accepted sense but rather manifestations of intense emotions, hopes and fears which these people were sensitive enough to intercept.

2

THINGS THAT GO BUMP

Paranormal phenomena encountered in haunted houses vary from gentle wraithes and delicious perfume to the ghostly apparition and horrifying sounds, strange noises, moving furniture, footsteps on the stairs and even the feel of cold hands on the face. My own home is haunted by a gentle Edwardian, whose presence is usually announced by the smell of coal-gas.

Other people are haunted by ghosts which are not quite so gentle, such as the young couple and their two children who moved into a council house in Hattersley during the early part of 1978. Unknown to them, the two-bedroomed, end terrace house had once been occupied by the moors murderers, Myra Hindley and Ian Brady.

Some fourteen years ago, an early-morning telephone-call from Hindley's brother-in-law alerted the local police that a murder had been committed there. A detective, posing as a bread-delivery man, managed to gain entrance to the house and found the body of Edward Evans, aged seventeen, in a bedroom. Later, together with other police officers, he found some photographs taken near the makeshift graves, high on the moors near Saddleworth, of Lesley Ann Downey, aged ten, and twelve-year-old John Kilbride. They also found tape-recordings of a frightened child's voice, which was later identified as that of Lesley Ann.

Hindley and Brady were brought to trial at Chester on 19th April 1966. Hindley was sentenced to two concurrent life sentences and a concurrent sentence of seven months, while Brady received three concurrent sentences of life imprisonment. After the trial and conviction, the house became known locally as 'the house of horror', and curiosity-seekers came from surrounding areas by bus and car, out of morbid curiosity, just to look at it. Later, the Manchester City Housing Committee re-let it, and two or three families moved in, although they never stayed very long.

The young couple in question had lived for several weeks in a homeless family unit and were overjoyed when they were informed that they had been allocated a two-bedroomed house at Hattersley. Unfortunately, no one thought to tell them the history of the house, and the address meant nothing to them. It was not until after they had moved in that people told them, "That's the moors murderers' house."

From the very beginning there was a strong feeling of evil, as if the presence of Hindley and Brady could still be felt. The night after the couple moved in, the house was burgled, and from then on, things gradually became worse: strange noises, creakings and groanings coming from upstairs, and at night mysterious tappings at the windows.

As soon as they knew that the house had been associated with Hindley and Brady, the couple contacted a priest, who blessed it, but still the presence persisted. Being young, they did not frighten very easily, but this house really gave them the creeps.

The area around Carnforth was ardently Quaker in the old days, and because of the Quakers' persecution and harassment, much of their suffering has been retained in the atmosphere of some of the old cottages hereabouts.

Mrs Burton, a widow, bought a seventeenth-century cottage in a pretty village near Carnforth in 1975. She began to renovate it, but in 1977, as a result of the following experiences, she decided to sell the house. In her letter to me of 19th April 1977, Mrs Burton told me that if she were not alone when the manifestations occurred, she could probably accept them.

When she first moved into the cottage, Mrs Burton was quite happy. She had expected to renovate it and settle down with her dog to the quiet and peace of the countryside, but gradually, over a period of twelve months, it became nerve-racking. Had she not lived alone, Mrs Burton would not have been unduly worried at the strange bangings and tappings that go on, or by the figures which appeared with regularity. Her dog, which, she tells me, is a wonderful guard-dog where humans are concerned, very often quakes with fright, his hair standing on end as if he has come into contact with a live electric cable, staring at something Mrs Burton cannot see, in the early hours of the morning.

At various times Mrs Burton saw at least four different phantoms. Most of the incidents seemed to take place upstairs. She was surprised to see two children playing there, and on another occasion she was met on the stairs by a small old lady in Victorian clothes. Across her shoulders she wore a blue cloak.

Because of these and other incidents, she decided to start sleeping downstairs on the settee, "which," she said, "seemed a little stupid, with two perfectly good bedrooms lying empty," but at least she had peace of mind – that is, until April 1977, when for no apparent reason she woke up at four o'clock one morning to see a woman carrying a child, gliding towards her across the room. She assured me that she was awake and that it was definitely not a dream.

I have found over the years that where there is almost definite proof of a haunting, the people concerned are usually a little reluctant to advertise the fact. Usually they try to find some rational explanation for their experiences rather than put it down to the supernatural. In time, however, even the most hardened sceptics can become convinced if the explanations runs out of credence.

Bank House, Haslingden, is the home of Rosemary and Alfred Stephens and their three children. It was built in 1886 for a Mr Parkinson, a local mill-owner and is a typical Victorian house, not unlike the old parsonage at Haworth in its layout, standing on high ground which falls away quite steeply and overlooking the mills and cottages not far away. On his death, old Mr Parkinson left the house to his children, with the proviso that it must always remain in the family. Over the years, members of the family either married or left the house for other reasons, and finally it was sold to the Stephens about six years ago.

When they bought the house, it was in a dilapidated condition, and there was no electricity, just gaslight, so the Stephens had electricity and central-heating installed. It was shortly afterwards that the mysterious happenings began. Mr Stephens told me, "We should have realized that there was something at the beginning, but we always tried to find a logical explanation for the things that happened – doors opening and closing by themselves, for instance."

Things disappeared and turned up again several days later. On a number of occasions, although the taps were turned off in the kitchen, the sink was full of water, and the floor was flooded. Footsteps were heard quite regularly, pacing the floor of an empty room, and they were also heard walking around the bed in Mr and Mrs Stephens' room. Unseen hands shook the bed; a child was heard sobbing and crying 'Mummy' during the night, and, although a search was made on each occasion, the sound evaded them. Other strange noises were heard, bangings and thumpings and what sounded like coal being tipped down a chute, somewhere at the rear of the house.

The first time anything was actually sighted was when Mrs Stephens went into one of the cellars and saw a footprint of a small child in a film of coal dust. At first she thought her daughter Naomi had been in the cellar, but, on checking the footprint with that of Naomi, it did not match at all. The footprint would have matched a child's size-four shoe, whereas Naomi was on a larger sized fitting. Another incident happened in the cellar, some time later....

For some unknown reason, every light in the house suddenly went out late one evening. Mark, the Stephens' sixteen-year-old son, went into the cellar to check the fuses. Mrs Stephens did not want him playing around with the fuses and went to the top of the cellar steps to call him back, while his father telephoned for an electrician. As she reached the steps, a 'boy' rushed up them towards her and, on reaching about arm's length, suddenly evaporated into thin air. Several seconds later Mark came up from the cellar, completely unaware of what had been going on.

Some time in 1976, Mrs Stephens was vacuuming upstairs when Naomi, who was six at the time, came running up to say that she had seen a man on the stairs. Thinking it was the gas-man, Mrs Stephens went onto the landing – to find it empty. She searched every room in the house but could find no-one. Naomi described the man as being dressed in a black suit, with white buttons and carrying a stick with a fancy top. (This appears to have been a silver-topped walking-cane.) She said that his face was all grey and that he had no eyes. According to Naomi, he disappeared into the bottom of the stairs.

Other incidents have occurred, as recently as the day before my visit to the house. Naomi swears that her mother goes into her room each night to kiss her and tuck her in, whereas Mrs Stephens only pops her head around the door to make sure that she is all right! There is a peculiar smell in the house sometimes, which Mrs Stephens says is rather like the smell of the old coal-gas.

The lady next door once accosted Mrs Stephens and asked whether

her husband had been beating her, for on the previous night the whole family had been kept awake for ages, listening to the terrible shouting and screaming coming from the house at about 1.30 am. Someone was shouting in one of the upstairs rooms: "Oh my God, you'll kill him. Leave him!" Strangely enough, the Stephens had slept through it all and heard nothing.

Mrs Stephens has seen at least two phantoms in the house: a woman dressed in black Victorian clothes once crossed the hall into the kitchen, and on another occasion an elderly woman, in more modern clothes, disappeared round the bannister. She told me, "I recognized her as a lady who had died not long before and who had been associated with the house in her younger days. At first I thought it was Naomi, but then as she turned the corner of the stairs, she sort of leaned on her knee with her hand, rather as an arthritic or old person would do when they climb stairs." She followed her, but on reaching the top the figure vanished.

A rather strange thing happened on the day I visited the Stephens to follow up this story.

Having spent some two hours discussing the phenomena, I asked if I might take a photograph of the front of the house. On receiving the prints from the processers, I was surprised to find that this particular print was covered in what appeared at first to be fogging. Closer examination showed that framed in the doorway was a very distinct human face, the face of an elderly Victorian gentleman, with a sharp nose, very deep-set eyes, side whiskers and beard. Mrs Stephens confirms this as describing the features of the figure seen by Naomi. Who it is we do not know, although we do know it is not the ghost of the late Mr Parkinson.

An old house in Sackville Street, in the Everton district of Liverpool, was haunted by a malignant ghost, who actually put a poor woman into hospital for some time.

The story goes that on the first night the family moved into the house, they were aware that something was amiss. A few friends had been invited to a small housewarming when, at about nine-thirty, someone became aware of footsteps moving about upstairs. A search revealed nothing but, fearing that a burglar was hiding upstairs, a couple of the men decided to run round to the local police-station to report it.

They had been gone only a few minutes when a cry was heard, followed by a loud thud. At the bottom of the stairs lay one of the guests in a dazed and confused state. On recovery the man said that he had been coming down the stairs when he felt what could only be described as two strong hands, picking him up by the waist and virtually throwing him down the stairs.

For several nights after this, the house was filled with strange noises, and the family decided that it might be better to sleep downstairs together, for safety and support. The next day, the men of the house set about moving the furniture from the bedrooms to the downstairs rooms. The lady previously mentioned followed them upstairs and was nearing the top when she cried out in terror. The men rushed to the landing and watched in horror as they saw her poised in the air. After a second or two she appeared to glide at great speed down the stairs, arms outstretched and surrounded by a haze. She landed on her feet and then appeared to be propelled with great force through the doorway of a room leading from the hall. The men rushed downstairs and found her in a faint. She was taken to hospital suffering from multiple injuries and shock.

No one knows what, or who, haunted the house in Sackville Street, nor what went on in the past. The haunting still remains a mystery.

A similar case cropped up in Lancaster a few years ago when a young couple, on getting married, moved into a house on Sibsey Street. It was a nice little house, which the couple took a great pride in decorating and furnishing to their taste.

One day, several months after moving in, the husband had left for work, and the wife, after dressing and making the bed, made to go downstairs. Looking down from the top of the stairs, she saw to her horror the body of a woman lying face down at their foot. Hardly believing what she saw, the young wife cautiously made her way down, and, as she did the body completely disappeared.

She was more puzzled than ever and not a little afraid that she might be suffering from some mental aberration. Later that day, when her husband returned home, she put the matter out of her mind.

Some weeks later, she was again coming down the stairs, this time later in the day, when she again saw the body lying exactly as she had seen it on the previous occasion, and again the vision vanished before she was able to reach the bottom of the stairs. By now she was convinced that she had seen a ghost and told her husband of her experiences when he arrived home later that evening. Her husband, a practical man, listened sympathetically but considered that she was perhaps tired and that her imagination was playing tricks on her.

A few weeks later, things came to a head. At about nine o'clock in the evening, the husband was reading the paper when he heard a startled cry and heard a bump on the stairs. Rushing out of the room he found his wife sitting on the bottom step rubbing a bruised ankle. She told him later that, as she was nearing the bottom step, she had noticed the woman's body again. The shock of seeing it so suddenly caused her to lose her footing and fall down the last couple of steps.

Her husband was by this time convinced that his wife had seen something unusual in the house, and was determined to find out about previous occupiers.

Some years previously, a young married couple, who were expecting their first child, moved into the house. The husband had been employed in shift work at Williamson's linoleum mills. While he was at work, his wife remained at home preparing for the happy event. One day, alas, she had slipped and fallen from the top of the stairs to the bottom, laying there quite dead, until her husband returned home that night and discovered the body.

The majority of modern hauntings are usually ascribed to the activities of poltergeists. The term 'poltergeist' is a compounded German word, meaning 'noisy spirit'. Though the reason for their appearance remains a mystery, poltergeists are probably the best-known of all current psychic phenomena. They are usually considered to be mischievous spirits which ring bells, break crockery, throw objects about and in general make nuisances of themselves.

They are not thought to be the spirits of the dead but rather an invisible form of energy occasioned by conditions of unresolved tension in the psyche of those who involuntarily produce them. We associate the activities of poltergeists with children in early adolescence, and, as the children grow older, so the activities gradually cease.

However, I am of the opinion that this theory is purely speculation, and I wonder whether these strange and often frightening manifestations are evidence of some other world which we have yet to explore.

Take the case of Mrs Audrey McDougal, a charming middle-aged lady who lives with her scientist husband and her son of twenty-four in a beautiful thirty-year-old house situated in a lovely quiet backwater at Read, near Burnley, overlooking St John's Church.

Two or three years ago, Mrs McDougal underwent a serious operation, and since then a series of strange incidents have occurred, which have been witnessed by all three members of the family.

It all began when Mrs McDougal came out of hospital. Quite a number of friends had sent her flowers, which she had arranged in a pewter coffee-pot on the fireplace in the lounge, with a few forsythia twigs. Later in the day, the family were all together in the lounge when suddenly a daffodil shot out of the coffee-pot and landed on the hearth-rug. It was immediately assumed the flower had been resting on a twig which had sprung, forcing it out of the pot, so Mrs McDougal re-arranged them and put the pot in the centre of the fireplace. On the following Monday, she went into the lounge to find another daffodil sitting on the chair beside the fireplace, several feet from the container.

On another occasion, the radio altered station, without any other person being present. Mrs McDougal said, "It was quite strange really. I keep the radio on to keep me company during the day, and I normally have a transistor on in the kitchen, but it was away being repaired. On this occasion I had to use the big radiogram in the dining-room. It sounded to me as if someone was quickly changing stations. I went into the dining-room, and the whole thing had been re-tuned. The radio has a vertical waveband, and the pointer was about two inches away from where I had originally tuned it." At the time she was the only person in the house.

Other strange things have happened. An ashtray on a small table flew across the room and landed beside the chair in which Mrs McDougal was sitting at the time. Pictures have moved of their own accord, and on one occasion Mrs McDougal watched, fascinated, as a large, heavy fire-screen in front of the fireplace began to waltz forward before tipping over onto the floor. A candle-holder has mysteriously transferred itself from a window-sill at one end of the room to a corresponding one at the other side, some fifteen feet away. Waste paper in her son's bedroom has been not only scattered on the floor but festooned over his dressing-table and wardrobe – all this while he was away at university.

Whatever is behind this mysterious power, it must use some force, for on one occasion a heavy bookcase was moved, one shelf being pulled out and placed across a room.

Mrs McDougal admitted that she often wakes up quite early in the mornings, because the room becomes quite cold. Because of her disability she has to sleep downstairs, and most mornings, even in the summer, she says she wakes up feeling extremely cold and has to get up to make a hot drink or fill a hot-water bottle.

Ghost or poltergeist? The house, so far as is known, is built on land belonging to the church, but there is no record of this land's having been used in the past for burials. It is interesting to speculate just what it is that is causing these disturbances, and, in view of the activities, one wonders whether Mrs McDougal is having trouble with a poltergeist or whether she has, in fact, a resident ghost.

A rather interesting ghost popped up on the Hunger Hill council estate in Bolton back in the early 1960s. A family moved into the house in 1958, and by November 1963, after five years of being plagued by ghosts, they decided they had had as much as they could take, and left.

It was not long after they had moved in that they began to hear bumping downstairs during the night. Although they investigated the noises several times, it was always impossible to identify the source. At first they did not think too much of the disturbances, but in time the thumping and banging became unbearable.

Other, even stranger, things began to happen, such as the 'bony figure' which climbed into the bed in which the parents slept; yet when they put their hands on the spot where the figure lay, there was nothing! When they switched on the light, the figure would vanish, but banging would emanate from the floorboards under the bed.

At other times, lights were turned off and on; objects would be thrown about the house by invisible hands, and the sound of footsteps could be heard, walking about the house at all times of day or night, stamping up and down the stairs. Several visitors suddenly left the house hurriedly, after invisible hands touched them, or when they felt something brush past them.

In October 1963 the ghost began to attack the children, two boys aged seven and eight and their sisters, aged eleven and seventeen. They began to complain of noises in the night and a 'presence' getting into bed with them. The boys said they were pinched by an invisible force and had their hair pulled. One night the parents were wakened by moaning and groaning coming from their seventeen-year-old daughter's room. Her father rushed in, to find her struggling to push some invisible being away from her. Later the girl said that a strange force seemed to have her in a stranglehold. By now the family was having very little sleep, and finally, one cold November night, the thumping and banging became so bad that the parents called a taxi, and the whole family left the house, spending the remainder of the night with a relative.

They refused to go back to the house after this and requested the Bolton Corporation housing-manager to find them alternative accommodation, because of the evil there. Bolton Corporation treated the matter seriously, much to their credit, and very soon the family were found another house, less than a mile away.

No one, so far as I can determine, was ever able to say what caused the house to be haunted. My own enquiries revealed that shortly after the house was built, sometime around 1925, there had been a case of suicide there. Whether or not this had any bearing on the frightening events that took place later, I have no idea. The house has since been re-let, and, although I was unable to interview the present tenants, discreet enquiries led me to believe that no one else seems to have been affected by these unusual hauntings.

If number 2, Dalton Square, Lancaster is not haunted, then it should be, for in September 1935 it was the scene of a terrible double murder, the like of which the old city had not witnessed for many a year.

This stone-built, three-storeyed terraced house, in the once fashionable square, was the residence of Dr Buck Ruxton, a highly respected Indian doctor, and his English wife, Isabella.

For reasons which are well documented elsewhere, Dr Ruxton murdered Isabella and was discovered dismembering her body in the bathroom, by their maid, Mary Rogerson. Alas, as a witness, poor Mary had to forfeit her life too. Both the bodies, after being dismembered, were wrapped in newspapers and taken in the boot of the doctor's car to Moffat, where they were thrown into a ravine.

In due course the bodies were found, still wrapped in the newspapers, one of which could only have been bought in Lancaster. Brilliant detective-work by the forensic laboratories and the Lancaster police eventually led them to the door of number 2, where Dr Ruxton was arrested and charged with the murder of Isabella and Mary.

Amid much publicity he was brought to trial at Manchester Crown Court, and after sentencing he was hanged at Strangeways.

The house has been empty for forty-three years at the time of writing, and no one will live in it. I am told that, up until fairly recently, there were still dirty, brownish marks in the bathroom, a silent reminder of that dreadful day in 1935.

Still in Lancaster, number 7 Church Street was the scene of a haunting. Church Street, lying in the shadow of the castle, is thought by many to be the site of an old Roman burial-ground, but, as far as I am aware, this has never been confirmed. Whether that, or the fact that the previous owner hanged himself from the bannister of the staircase, has any bearing on the disturbances at number 7, one cannot be sure.

The premises have now been demolished, and on the site there stands a new shopping-precinct. Not so long ago, however, this was the home and business premises of Mr and Mrs C. Bowker.

Although they never saw anything, they knew that the flat above the shop was haunted, because of the strange goings-on which occurred almost nightly: shuffling footsteps up and down the stairs and along the landings, doors being opened and then closing by themselves, sometimes all night long. Mrs Bowker said that the previous owner had had a dog, and she herself often experienced the feeling that, at some time during the night, an animal of some kind had jumped on the bed. She did emphasize that at no time at all did the family feel any hostility towards them, and they never felt afraid.

A similar case was brought to my attention a short time ago near Burnley. Leaving Burnley and driving towards Padiham, one passes the lovely old All Saints' Church at Habergham. Between the churchyard and the school nestles the little school house, which for years belonged to the Shuttleworth family of nearby Gawthorpe Hall and which later became the home of successive school caretakers.

During the latter part of the 1940s young Arthur Brown lived here with his parents, his father having obtained the positions of caretaker at the school and part-time grave-digger at the church. The old school house was haunted by a mischievous ghost which moved things and which appeared to centre itself around Arthur. Sometimes, when he was in bed, the room would suddenly grow cold, and a mysterious force would shake his bed quite fiercely. His parents, too, heard the noises made by the shaking of the bed and the mysterious happenings which occurred from time to time, but, of course, having younger children, they deemed it wise to try to cover up the happenings, for fear of causing them distress.

Gradually the whole family, including the children, became used to the strange goings-on and came to accept them, although the present Mrs Brown, who at the time was still courting Arthur, told me that all the time the family lived at the school house, she could never be persuaded to go upstairs – not, she assures me, that she knew about the ghost, but for some reason she is unable quite to understand.

A ghost turned up in the Digmoor area of Skelmersdale New Town in 1968 which scared the daylights out of the residents. Footsteps were heard when no one was about, accompanied by sudden drops in temperature, even in centrally heated homes. One man was on the verge of returning to Liverpool with his family, after only two weeks in his new home. As it was, he gave up a good job at a local factory, which involved shift work, so that he could remain at home at nights with his terrified wife. Another family living nearby called in a priest to exorcize apparitions in their reasonably new home. To this day no one has been able to explain these hauntings.

Nor can anyone explain away the ghost of the old sailor who haunted the Liverpool seamen's home for nearly a century. As a seafarer myself, I spent many nights there during the late 1950s and heard many tales of this ghost. Although I personally did not see it, I spoke to many members of staff and a few sailors who claimed they had.

Unexplained footsteps were often heard; doors would open as if by themselves, and on several occasions a man dressed in the clothes of a nineteenth-century seaman has been seen, sitting beside a fireplace in one of the communal rooms. Alas, this place no longer remains; a new building has replaced it at the Pier Head. The ghost was thought to be that of an old sea-dog who, having retired from the sea, spent his remaining days at the home, where he subsequently died. But that is pure supposition.

3

SPECTRAL WORKMATES

The premises of the Broad Oak Printing Works at Accrington contain a friendly ghost, with an ice-cold grip, which has frightened a number of workmen.

The works were rebuilt in 1926, and some people think it could be the ghost of an old printing employee of several years ago, while others are convinced it is the ghost of a lonely old man who used to work there and who always wanted to talk in the company of workmates. To make them stay and listen, he had developed the habit of holding on to their arms as he spoke.

During the fire brigade strike of 1977, volunteers were recruited by the firm who now occupy the premises, to assist the night watchman in fire-watching. One such man, a down-to-earth, thirty-six-year-old tradesman's mate, who was not the type of person to believe in ghosts, experienced something which was to change his mind a few minutes after midnight, one Saturday early in January 1978.

The man was walking down the main aisle of the splitting department, whistling to himself as he checked that everything was in order, when he suddenly felt a rush of cold air, and had a feeling that someone was creeping up on him from behind. As the hairs at the back of his neck began to rise, to his horror, a hand gently took hold of his arm. It was very cold, and he could feel the thumb and fingers pressing gently. Looking down and seeing nothing, he was overtaken by fear and, turning on his heels, raced back to find the night-watchman.

After several cups of coffee, the shaken man began to calm down and explain to the watchman what had frightened him. They decided that the following night they would investigate together.

On the next night, Sunday, after checking that no machinery or fans were running, the two men set up a tape-recorder in the splitting department, and just before midnight they switched on and returned to the night-watchman's office to await results. The play-back was amazing. The noises that came out of the recorder were of machinery which sounded rather like an old loom or plating machine. There was also a loud ticking noise like that of an old pendulum clock. The recording does not, however, sound anything like any of the machinery used in the splitting room at the present day.

Other workers report experiencing a strange atmosphere in this room and have had the feeling that there has been someone watching them, as if wanting to make contact.

Another factory ghost pops up at Standish, near Wigan. Over a period of about four years, several unexplained happenings at this Standish mill culminated in a rather bizarre incident one night late in 1963, causing a nineteen-year-old cloth-roller at the old mill to faint with shock while working on the back shift.

On his recovery, he said that he had looked up from his machine and seen a figure in a long coat floating in the air a couple of feet from the factory floor. The phantom wore old-fashioned knickerbockers and seemed to have a white scarf wound around its neck.

Although he did not know it, the terrified worker had seen the ghost of Rev. Charles Newton Hutton, who had been rector of Standish for fifty years and who had died in 1938. Older Standish residents still remember him to this day, short-necked, bearded and invariably wearing gaiters. Even today the old rector's ghost is believed to haunt the village, although, I am assured, he is harmless enough. Apparently, the mill was erected on land which belonged to the rectory, and Rev. Hutton had had a financial interest in it when it was first built. During his lifetime he was a frequent visitor to the mill.

There is an odd twist to this story, for, by a remarkable coincidence, the appearance of the apparition to the mill machinist occurred the day before the Rev. Hutton's widow died!

When the Co-operative Stores closed down in Albert Road, Colne, it caused quite a stir in those parts, for it had stood on that site for as long as folk around there could remember, catering for everything from meat to haberdashery; it was inconceivable that anyone would think of holding a wedding reception or funeral tea anywhere but at the Co-op. It stood as a proud symbol of the wealth of the Co-operative Movement in those parts, and to work there, years ago, was to be looked upon as someone who was 'going places', so particular were they in their choice of staff.

Behind the main Co-op building stands Colne Hall, an ugly Victorian building which started life as a manor house, graduated to a beer hall and finally became part of the Co-operative complex. The boiler-room and other parts of the Hall are reputed to be haunted by the ghost of a young girl, who has appeared quite suddenly on many occasions and a minute or so later has vanished into thin air, just as quickly. She is said to be wearing the clothes typical of those worn by poorer children in this part of the county towards the end of the last century.

Other incidents and noises have been observed in this building, and as recently as early 1978, members of staff of 'Princess of Norway', a furnishing and fabrics firm which now owns the building, reported seeing and hearing things which they are hard-put to explain. A young woman who works there told me that doors open by themselves; footsteps are heard in places were no human being is present, and, she says, she has often had the feeling of not being alone when no one else is in the room with her.

A close friend of ours who has worked for many years at the Co-op told me that she has in fact seen the ghost. On one occasion she was startled to see the distinct figure of a little girl, in old-fashioned clothes, walk straight past her. She watched for several seconds before the figure disappeared.

She told me that one old caretaker, now retired, often saw this figure in the boiler room. It would suddenly appear beside him as if watching him stoke the boiler and would vanish just as quickly. On one occasion, she remembered, someone brought a dog into the building which showed signs of fear when its owner tried to take it up one particular staircase.

Who was the sad little girl whose ghost roams the building, and why does she appear? Was she perhaps a pauper child, brought from the South to labour and finally perish in the new factories that sprang up in these parts over a century ago, or could she have any connection with the poor deranged soul who murdered her three children in the area in 1887?

Sometime in 1969 a gang of demolition men arrived in Southport to pull down the old Palace Hotel. They thought it would be a straight-forward job to rig up scaffolding, contact the electricity, gas and water authorities to have supplies cut off and then remove the interior fittings before dismantling the building itself. They had done it many times before with the minimum of fuss, and there was no reason to believe that the Palace Hotel would be any different from the other demolition jobs they had undertaken. However, things were soon to prove quite otherwise.

One man, quietly dismantling upstairs in a corridor, did not feel too happy because the atmosphere seemed to him to be a little eerie, but, of course, all old buildings were like this when they were empty; he had been in hundreds. Suddenly he heard whispering nearby, but when he looked up, no one was about. The whispering continued for some time as he hurriedly finished his job and left the corridor.

The biggest mystery, though, concerned the lift. Although the power had been cut off, the lift would suddenly and inexplicably begin to ascend and descend of its own accord. One day a group of demolition men entering the hotel foyer were surprised to see the lift doors suddenly close and the car ascend to the second floor. Thinking that someone was playing tricks on them, the men ran up to the winding room and were astonished to find that the lift brake was still in the 'on' position, which should have prevented the lift from moving at all. To forestall any further tricks being played on them, the men cut the lift cables, thus hoping to send the car crashing to the bottom of the shaft. To their amazement, the car stayed where it was at the second floor and refused to budge.

The shaken men set about cutting through the shafts, and finally heavy hammers were employed until, several hours later, the car plunged to the bottom, burying itself several feet into the floor.

The hotel had in the past been subject to all sorts of happenings: no dog would pass a certain corridor, and research revealed that, many years before, a man had committed suicide there. At other times the hotel had been used to shelter and care for victims of a sea tragedy, and some of the unfortunates had indeed died there.

Now the hotel is gone, and presumably the ghosts with it. Who or what they were, we shall probably never know. Soon the Palace Hotel will be forgotten entirely, but while ever demolition men gather together, this story will continue to be told, throughout the length and breadth of Britain.

A similar mysterious presence haunts an 'electrical superstore' in Burnley.

There has been a chapel on Bethesda Street in the centre of Burnley for over 150 years. Alongside the present Unitarian Church there, and bordering close to St James' Street, was the graveyard. Sometime during the 1950s the old Sunday school was pulled down, and the graveyard was built over, until today the church stands sandwiched between a block of offices on one side and the electrical superstore on the other. Could the fact that the superstore is haunted have anything to do with the fact that it is built on the site of the graveyard, and that local people are of the opinion that, unknown to the developers, some bodies had been buried in the old Sunday school building and may have been left disinterred?

Prior to the opening of the store in July 1978, rumours began to circulate that things were not quite what they should be. When a fitter was repairing a window at the front of the store, alone at the time – no other person was in the building, he heard voices coming from a storeroom. The voices were muffled, and he was unable to make out what was being said, but on investigation he was startled to discover that there was no one there. Returning to the front of the shop, he was even more amazed to discover that all the doors had been locked behind him! Gas and electricity workers also complained of inexplicable happenings, and people began to feel that there was definitely something odd about the place.

It was enough to disturb anyone who went into the building, let alone the staff who work there at the present time. Alarm-bells ring after they have been turned off; light-bulbs appear from nowhere and smash on the floor; the lift stops quite suddenly for no apparent reason, and no electrical fault can be discovered which might cause this to happen.

The biggest scare came in July 1978, when three receptionists in the front shop heard a terrific crash coming from a small storeroom. The door was locked, so it was impossible for there to be anyone in there. On investigating, two smashed light-bulbs were found on the floor. This being an electrical store, one would not suppose this to be an unusual occurrence: after all, they could have fallen from the shelves. One thing puzzled the investigators though, for, as one young member of the staff said, "The type of bulbs that were smashed were pre-war and unlike anything that is sold today!" The staff do not know to this day where the bulbs came from. When the manager went to check the boiler room which leads off from the storeroom, another of these pre-war bulbs was seen to roll, as if from nowhere, into the middle of the floor. Another noticeable fact is that the temperature is markedly lower in this small storeroom than in any other part of the building, when in fact everywhere should be of a constant temperature.

On another occasion, when the storeroom door was opened, it was discovered that a vacuum hose and a calculator had been moved. It is certain that no member of staff had been in there, and the most mystifying thing of all is that when someone went to pick it up, the vacuum hose was red hot!

While in the Burnley area, mention should be made of the ghost which was said to have haunted the Bull Street premises of the *Burnley Express and News*.

Edward Fishpool, from a sea-faring family, widely read and speaking five languages, left his native Middlesbrough in 1909 to work for a short while on a newspaper in Blackburn. In 1910 he moved to Burnley with his family and about this time joined the *Burnley Express* as a printer.

Printer's ink replaced the blood in his veins. He had been in the printing trade since leaving school and had travelled the world delivering newspaper machinery.

In May 1928, at the age of sixty-four, Ned, as he was known, was given the job of supervising the removal of machinery from the *Express* to Retford in Nottinghamshire. However, earlier in the week he had become ill with pneumonia and was, in the event, unable to see the job through. Ned was devoted to the *Express*, and the machinery meant everything to him. His dearest wish was to remove it, and, I am told, there were tears on his cheeks when he died a few days later, because he had not been able to fulfil his obligations.

Since his death, Ned's ghost has been seen a couple of times at the Bull Street premises, usually on a balcony of the machine room. He was spotted for the first time, early in the 1930s, by an overseer who had worked under him in his youth.

After this, whenever there was a breakdown in the printing machinery, or when the machinery did strange things for no apparent reason, it was always considered that 'Old Ned' had been involved in some way.

Every St Helens resident knows that Croppers Hill, on the Prescot Road, used to be called 'Combshop Brow'. Until the last quarter of last century, a cottage with a large garden stood at the right-hand side of the road, near to the top of the hill, for many years occupied by an old comb-maker, famous throughout the district for the excellent quality of his wares. Being the only building situated on the brow, this old cottage gave its name to the locality, and for many years 'Combshop Brow' was the only name by which it was known.

At the bottom of Croppers Hill stood the Engineers' Hall, with a gateway flanked on each side by brick buildings, one of which was used as a private residence, while the other was a gatehouse to one of the factories behind it.

For a number of years there had been stories told of mysterious happenings and strange appearances of ghostly figures visible from time to time on the premises, but it was on Wednesday, 24th September 1875, at about three o'clock in the afternoon, that the crisis arose. An industrious glass-engraver quietly working in a room partitioned off from the first floor of the lodge, suddenly heard a shower of stones come crashing through the front windows of the building. Rushing outside, he found an excited crowd of several hundred people assembled in the road. In vain, the manager tried to drive the mob away and stop the stone-throwing, but the crowd would not move on. Dozens of them claimed they had seen a ghost at the window and wanted another view. Meanwhile, as an occasional discharge of missiles was still kept up, the workmen inside began to fix up boards against the windows to stop the entrance of stones and to prevent any further damage. More and more people arrived at the scene, and eventually the police had to be called to restore order and clear the road.

For several days afterwards, passers-by and local people claimed that the place was haunted and that they could see a ghostly face at the window. From time to time stones were thrown at the windows until virtually every pane of glass had been broken. Gradually the excitement died away, but the broken windows remained shuttered for years after the factory had closed down, bearing witness to an occurrence which has never yet been satisfactorily explained. Today the area around Croppers Hill is still reputed to be haunted.

Close to Manchester Airport are the offices of Claridge and Co., a leading freight-forwarding company. The building used by this firm in fact houses several companies, but it is only the offices of Claridge's that appear to be affected by an apparition that has been seen several times since it made its first appearance in 1971.

The building was originally the barrack block of 613 Manchester Squadron of the Royal Air Force, and it is thought that the ghost may be connected, but people who have seen it, mainly cleaners and late-working clerical staff, describe the phantom as 'an old man'.

Police were called once, when screams and other noises were heard coming from the empty offices, and equipment was found to have been moved. On another occasion screams were heard early one morning, followed by the sound of footsteps in the corridors. One of the company's clerks saw the figure of an old man sitting in the storeroom next to his office, but when he opened the dividing door to speak to him, the figure vanished.

A few nights later he was seen again, by one of the night staff, who described him as "an old man who walked through the office in his bare feet". Other witnesses to the apparition have been a lorry-driver and a policeman, but as yet no one has been able to identify him.

Penny Lane was well-known among Merseysiders long before the Beatles made it world-famous.

Two printers who own the premises at 44, Penny Lane heard strange noises, one weekend, coming from their empty shop. They could find no explanation. This went on for several weeks, usually at weekends. Neighbours, thinking that vandals had broken in, called the police, who, after a thorough check of the premises, admitted themselves baffled. No explanation can be given for the banging and shuffling of this unseen ghost, who is thought to be that of a previous tenant.

The noises have been tape-recorded after the floorboards were removed, and roof, walls, furniture and equipment have been checked, but no evidence of his identity has been obtained so far.

When workmen were demolishing the old Royalty Theatre at the top of Cheapside, Morecambe, they were surprised to hear ghostly organ-music coming from the area around the stage. A number of men refused to work there alone.

Having demolished the theatre, the speculators moved in and built a shopping precinct on the site. One of the shops, currently leased by a television dealer, stands just about on the spot where the old Royalty stage once stood, and I am told that the room at the back of the shop has a weird and eerie atmosphere about it. Although the staff do not like working in the back, they have never seen anything, but one of the girls told me, "There is certainly a presence of some kind. It is as if we are being watched by unseen eyes."

On several occasions, they too have heard the ghostly music, but no one is able to come up with an explanation.

As a matter of interest, there is an office in Peter Street, in the heart of Manchester, where many people have heard phantom pipes playing over the past few years. Who or what the phantom flautist is, no one knows. Nor can anyone recognize the thin piping tune, which does not sound like music of the present day.

An evil presence is threatening the friendly, haunted atmosphere of 'Studio Arts', an art gallery in Cheapside, Lancaster, whose premises date back to 1720. For years now, the staff have become quite used to the benign spirit who gives off a strong aroma of lavender water and tobacco. He even ruffled the hair of one member of the staff and breathed down the neck of another, yet no one was frightened of him.

But now, another, less pleasant spirit has moved in, and the people at the gallery are worried in case it frightens away the friendly ghost. Doors mysteriously close on members of staff; pictures move, and there is a frightening atmosphere in the part of the gallery where a number of Lowry paintings are kept.

No one knows the identity of either of the two spirits, but it is thought that they may have something to do with a man who murdered his wife there many years ago and who was hanged at Lancaster Castle. But no one knows whether he is the friendly ghost, or whether the murderer has suddenly appeared. Perhaps it is his wife who objects to his paying too much attention to the attractive young ladies who work there!

Her Majesty's Prison at Liverpool possesses not a spectral workmate but a spectral cell-mate, for many prisoners prefer solitary confinement rather than to stay in cell G2, once occupied by William Kennedy, who murdered an Essex policeman in 1927. Kennedy was hanged at Walton, and ever since, his ghost has haunted this cell, in which he is said to have spent the period from his trial until his execution. Many a hard-case prisoner is said to have begged to be moved out after awakening in the middle of the night to find the gaunt spectre of William Kennedy peering at him in the gloom.

The lecture theatre at Burnley Central Library has a ghost which has been heard to play the piano.

A librarian is said to have been working late one evening after the library had closed, when suddenly, from the lecture-theatre above the main library, he heard the strains of classical music being played on a piano. Thinking that a member of the public had found his way in there, he went up to demand an explanation and was amazed to find the lecture theatre empty and the piano apparently playing by itself. The phenomenon has been reported several times since.

It is thought that the ghost is from one of the old houses which occupied the site, prior to the library's being built in 1929. I understand that, several years before the site was developed, a particularly gruesome murder was committed hereabouts, but whether this has any connection with the phantom pianist, I do not know.

Our final ghost in this section pops up at the new Skelmersdale Sports Centre, which was opened early in 1978 and which boasts a spectral black-cloaked figure. Amplifiers refuse to work, and the lights fail for no apparent reason. Local suggestions are that the building of such a centre on this site has offended a spirit from the past, though whom and why, nobody knows.

4

HAUNTED HOSTELRIES

Many inns and public houses in England are reputed to be haunted; just how many actually are is open to debate. Many of our hostelries go back a long way in history and were the focal point in community life, particularly that of a village.

Most people prefer their spirits out of the optic, but if, like myself, the reader is interested in the other kind of spirit too, then the two hobbies can be combined in a most delightful way. The following guide to our haunted pubs and inns is by no means comprehensive, but I am sure most readers will find them well worth a visit.

'The Ring o' Bells', Middleton, Manchester, is haunted by a Cavalier of the Civil War period, a rather sad-looking ghost, dressed in a plumed hat, lace collar and cloak and carrying a sword. Footsteps have been heard in the cellars, which date back to Norman times, and not so many years ago the flagstones were dug up, and helmets and weapons were found beneath them, dating from the Civil War. Some human bones were also found, which are thought to be the bones of a Royalist who was killed there by the Parliamentarians, and whose ghost now haunts the pub.

The Shakespeare Hotel in Fountain Street, in the centre of Manchester, is an ancient inn where most of the city's visiting show-business personalities gather. This old pub is haunted by the ghost of a servant-girl who, about a hundred years ago, was killed after her clothes caught fire in the kitchen. In her panic she rushed to the top of the stairs before being overcome and falling headlong to her death. Her ghost has been seen on a number of occasions by both staff and guests.

'Blighty's', at Farnworth, is built on the site of a cemetery, but its ghost is thought to be that of a former member of staff. Both staff and customers have often been surprised to see the unexplained figure of an elderly woman polishing tables, which disappears when approached. Strange, shimmering lights have been seen, apparently hovering in front of the stage; unusual noises have emanated from empty rooms, and lights have been mysteriously switched off and on.

Also at Farnworth, the Dixon Green Labour Club is haunted by a ghost known as 'The Blue Lady'. She is said to be a most beautiful ghost of a girl in her early twenties, with long golden hair tied with a bow, wearing a flowing blue dress with puffed sleeves and surrounded by the delicious rustle of silk as she moves. She is thought to have been a victim of the Civil War, and the sight of her is considered to bode ill for the residents.

The Irwell Castle Hotel in Salford is the haunt of a strange, shadowy ghost which looks like a person as seen through frosted glass. The figure is said to be about five feet six inches tall and indistinguishable, but seen quite frequently coming in through the back of the hotel.

Across the other side of Manchester, at the Olde Rock House, Barton-on-Irwell, there is a ghost of a country yokel thrashing a flail and muttering, "Now Thus, Now Thus", the motto of the de Trafford family. According to legend, one of the de Traffords, fleeing Cromwell's troops, ran into a barn, grabbed a farmer's smock and put it on (along with an appropriate country bumpkin expression) and joined the corn-threshing. Whether or not the disguise worked, I cannot say. However, some years ago, a flail and a pile of old clothes were found in a recess under the attic floor of the inn and were exhibited in a glass case as a reminder of the de Trafford whose ghost is still sighted from time to time, muttering, "Now Thus, Now Thus".

Now over to Bolton and the Wood Street Labour Club, said to be haunted by a pair of Victorian lovers. The club occupies what was once the home of the late William Lever, who was born there in 1851. Footsteps and other inexplicable noises have been heard many times, but it is the two ghosts which provide the most interest, for they appear to be a couple in their thirties, who materialize at a table near the door, holding hands. They seem to be very happy and obviously very much in love, for they have eyes for no one but each other. 'He' is a clean-shaven man, who wears a Victorian frock coat and cravat, while his companion wears a long, dark-coloured dress and bustle.

A man hanged himself in the cellars of the Radcliffe Arms Inn at

Oldham many years ago, and his spectre now roams the pub. I am told that this ghost has materialized at least once as a customer, quietly drinking a pint of his favourite ale.

On the road leading from the top of Blackstone Edge to Rochdale, stands the Rake Inn. ('Rake' is a local expression for a rough track leading to the moors, and is nothing to do with the ghost.) This hostelry boasts a genial ghost, a handsome Cavalier with uproarious laughter and laughing, twinkling eyes. He possibly has some connection with a nearby cottage known as 'Oliver's Cottage', in which Cromwell is said to have spent the night.

Over in Waterfoot in the Rossendale valley stands the Railway Inn, which boasts a ghost whose footsteps are heard during the night and where they have regular visits from a tall ghostly lady, dressed in grey.

Not very far away is the Griffin Hotel at Haslingden, haunted by an old lady. Who she is, no one knows, but she seems to be quite a mischievous old girl. Mrs Holden, the landlady, told me that one night, at about one-thirty or so, she was sitting upstairs reading when she heard pop music blaring out downstairs. She thought at first that some youths were playing a transistor radio out in the street and on looking out of the window was surprised to see no one about. She then realized that the music was coming from the bar of her pub. Mrs Holden went down to the bar and, to her amazement, found the juke-box lit up and a Shirley Bassey record just coming to an end.

Another curious incident happened the day I visited the pub. A young man was standing quietly at the bar when, for no apparent reason, his glass shattered, showering him with beer!

Over to the Accrington area now, and 'The Bridge House' at Hapton. This old pub stands beside the Leeds and Liverpool canal, and behind it the old bargees had a yard and stable, sometimes used as a temporary mortuary for bodies fished out of the canal. A local girl, many years ago, committed suicide by jumping from the canal bridge and has since returned to haunt the pub. This pathetic ghost has been seen by successive landlords, going up the steps leading to the pantry.

'The Black Bull' at Huncoat, reputed to have been a stopping-off point for some of Cromwell's troops in need of refreshments, is haunted by a presence which seems to follow people on the stairs. Nothing has been seen, but the bar service-bells are known to ring during the night, for no apparent reason.

It is but a short drive from Huncoat to Padiham and the Royal British Legion Club, where there is a ghost in an upstairs room, which has been seen by several people, including the club secretary and the steward. A shadow is often seen flitting across an upstairs landing and disappearing into a large disused room. After the phenomenon has been seen, the door leading to this particular room is found to be swinging slightly. Things are known to disappear and re-appear again in a different spot. No one seems to know the cause of the haunting, but whoever he is, the ghost seems to be friendly.

'Smackwater Jack's', off Hargreaves Street in Burnley, used to be an old iron and steel warehouse. It was closed down for about six or seven years and remained empty until it was bought in 1977, when work commenced on converting it into an Edwardian-style wine-bar. As workmen were putting the finishing touches to it, one of the owners who was sitting in his office when he heard footsteps coming down an old stairway. As the workmen had finished for the day, he thought someone might have stayed behind, but on investigation, no one could be found. Since then the footsteps have been heard quite often, and female members of the staff will go upstairs to the offices or the lounge only in pairs. The locals tell me that this ghost is probably that of a young warehouse worker who died on these premises during the last century. Although he has been heard clomping down the stairs, he has never been seen.

Foulridge, near Colne, traditionally got its name during the Civil War, when a general is said to have remarked, "This is a foul ridge upon which to fight a battle!" In reality the name is less romantic, for it really means 'ridge where foals graze' and derives from the Old English. The New Inn at Foulridge has a ghost which is believed to be connected with a Cavalier who died in conflict hereabouts. Others, myself included, think it is connected with the old Quakers' Meeting House and its burial ground nearby, for gravestones from this burial-ground were used to form part of an adjoining wall, although the remains of the interred were not disturbed.

During the 1960s a number of renovations were carried out at the inn, and since then successive landlords and families have been troubled with footsteps during the night and mysterious knocks on the bedroom door. Many years ago, a small bedroom at the back of the

inn was affected by a large luminous cross, which would form on the ceiling of the room even when the curtains were closed and the room was in darkness.

We will now head west across to the Clitheroe area and the Punch Bowl Inn at Hurst Green where we meet the well-known spectre of the legendary Ned King, highwayman, who confined his talents to the area between Longridge and Clitheroe, making 'The Punch Bowl' his headquarters. Here, from the safety of the hayloft above the barn, he could size up his potential victims, moneyed gentlemen and their ladies, as they alighted from their coach. After being refreshed, the victims would return to their coach, and, as they drove away, Ned King, Knight of the High Toby, would be waiting for them with pistols drawn, a mile or so down the road. Having robbed them, King made his escape across the fields, back to 'The Punch Bowl'. Eventually his luck ran out, and the troopers finally caught up with him in his hide-out above the barn. He shot it out for a while, but eventually the troopers caught him in what is now approximately the right-hand corner of the minstrel's gallery, and overpowered him, putting him in chains.

Poor Ned was never brought to trial but was hanged from a gibbet not far from the front door of the old inn, a spot past which he must have galloped on his way to and from his many hold-ups.

For well over 150 years his ghost has haunted 'The Punch Bowl'. Although the hauntings are less frequent now, unexplained moaning can often be heard among the rafters. Noises are heard in the corridors at dead of night, and bottles unaccountably fall from shelves.

The Sun Inn a few miles away at Chipping is haunted by the ghost of Lizzie Dean, a serving-wench who, in the 1850s, committed suicide after being left at the altar. Shortly after moving into the inn, the present landlord became aware of unusual happenings. Sweeping up the hallway and called away for a few moments, when he returned, the cigarette ends and dust he had left in a pile had disappeared, and the brush was on the opposite side of the hallway from where he had left it. He saw Lizzie's ghost after that on several occasions. One day, in the main bar he saw a cloudy figure, wearing a long dress with balloon sleeves, hair swept up on the top of her head, walk from the tap-room into the main bar, through a wall. Sometime later, it was decided to make a hatch in the wall through which the figure had passed, and when the work was started, a door over two hundred years old was discovered concealed in the stone work. This was originally the door to some steps leading to a drinking room – a door through which Lizzie would have passed frequently, to and from the kitchen.

Let us now retrace our steps to Merseyside and the west coast, where the Adelphi Hotel in Liverpool's Lime Street is haunted by a friendly phantom. One girl who worked there recently told me that she woke up, at about 5 am on her first night at the hotel, to find the figure of a man standing by her bed. At the time she was very frightened but was told at breakfast, "It was only George." She said, "I have found out since that he is really quite friendly, but he is rather nosy." No one seems to know who he is or what causes his visitations – perhaps he just likes pretty girls.

The Punch Bowl Inn at Sefton is said to be haunted by a seaman who died during the reign of Queen Elizabeth I. The mist-enshrouded head and shoulders of a young man have been seen floating several feet from the ground. Other people have seen a figure of a man dressed in sea-faring clothes, sitting in a corner by the fireplace at the rear of a ground-floor room. Apparently this room was used years ago as a mortuary for the bodies of sailors washed ashore, prior to their burial in Sefton churchyard; it is thought the ghost could be one of these drowned sailors.

The Stanley Arms Inn at Eccleston, St Helens, boasts a ghost which is described as being of the spectral bridegroom type, and known locally as 'the Gillars Green Ghost' – some poor unfortunate man who returns to the scene of some long-forgotten tragedy.

Mid-way between St Helens and Wigan, in the village of Billinge, stands the Stork Hotel which is haunted by the ghost of a rowdy Cavalier. This ghost has been seen within the last year or two, moving around the pub, stamping his feet, walking up and down stairs and sending glasses hurtling from the bar. The story behind this ghost is that a Cavalier died in the cellars of the pub when it was used as a prison during the Civil War. A customer is reputed to have been washing his hands in the 'gents'' when he saw a Cavalier stand beside him. The customer, who came from out of town and did not know of the ghost, thought there was a fancy-dress party going on.

Another ghost associated with the Stork Hotel is that of Jack Lyon, the last known highwayman, who was one of the hotel's most infamous guests. It is said that his ghost rides a horse through Billinge in the after-midnight hours. Sounds of cantering hooves can be heard; a popular footpath has been churned up by horse's hooves, and an early-morning motorist claims to have seen the mounted phantom.

Five miles away, in Wigan, 'The Minorca' is reported as having a ghost who pulls his own beer. This seventeenth-century inn, in the centre of town, has seen several mysterious happenings over the past few years. The ghost has been seen to pass through locked doors, to interfere with the tape-recorder used to play music in the bar and to pull itself a pint of beer, even when the pumps have been turned off for the night. However, perhaps he does not like this particular brew, for although the ghost draws himself a glass, it is never consumed.

Historic Park Hall Leisure Centre at Charnock Richard was for many years the home of the de Hoghtons, who during Elizabethan times sheltered priests on the run from the authorities. Monks met ladies in secluded woods; secret trysts took place in secret passages; plots and counter-plots were hatched. Legend has it that the ghost of a monk roams the grounds, seeking his lost lady-love. But Park Hall's most spectacular ghost is that of the mysterious white lady who rises out of the centre of the large lake in front of the building and has been seen by several people. Mysterious and unexplained footsteps are very often heard in the area around the banqueting hall, but the lady of the lake has not been seen in recent years.

Up the coast now to Lytham and 'The Ship and Royal', where there have been a number of curious incidents over the years. The ghost, nicknamed 'Charlie', has tampered with files, moved papers and even telephoned the meat suppliers, using the telephone answering-service to place an order for meat. A tall, dark, eerie figure of a man has been seen by staff at the far end of the grill on the second floor, and also by customers on several occasions. Theory has it that this is the ghost of the late squire, John Clifton, who died at Tenerife in 1928 and who pops in to visit his favourite local periodically.

Over on the Kirkham by-pass stands 'The Bell and Bottle' which is rumoured to be haunted after two killings took place there many years ago. One apparition is said to haunt a corridor, while another is said to be the ghost of a stable-boy who was kicked to death by a horse, in what is today the restaurant.

Blackpool's famous 'Lobster Pot' has a rather cheeky ghost who is quite partial to waitresses. Strangely enough, this ghost seems to be active only on Tuesdays and Wednesdays, and only in one particular part of the restaurant. Waitresses are grabbed by the arm or leg, and although he remains unseen, red finger-marks on arms and legs are ample evidence of his mischief. Who or what this ghost is, no one knows.

The Rooftree Inn at Middleton Sands, near Morecambe, had a landlord who reported seeing 'a grey lady' in the bar some years ago. So far as is known, she has not been seen for a number of years now.

Another authenticated grey lady has been seen on a number of occasions at the Clarendon Hotel on Morecambe's West End promenade. Who she is, no one knows. 'The Clarendon' was built on ground which had been designated as the site for a church, and some people think the ground may have been consecrated, which may account for the haunting, but I agree with those who link the ghost with someone who committed suicide there some years ago. It is more than likely to be that ghost which now haunts the first-floor corridors.

A little further down the promenade stands the Midland Hotel, built by the old Midland Railway Company. Here they have an unusual ghost, which has caused many a night porter to resign on the spot. During the Second World War, the hotel was requisitioned by the RAF as a hospital for officers, and the cellars were used as a mortuary. An ex-porter told me that when he was on duty one night, he saw a wraith-like figure, its features and outlines indistinct, glide through the doors leading from the cellars and make its silent way to the lift. To his horror, the lift doors closed, and the lift set off to the second floor. Another porter told me of having been sitting in reception and hearing the lift coming. He looked up to see who it was coming down at that late hour and was terrified when the lift stopped, the doors opened and revealed an empty lift car. He refused to work nights after that, and it was not long before he resigned.

Towards the end of 1946, my parents took on the position of steward and stewardess of the Skerton Liberal Club, a lovely old Georgian building in Lune Street, Lancaster. Since their time, the club has undergone extensive alterations, but in those days the committee rooms and one of the billiard rooms were situated on the first floor, along with our own accommodation. This first-floor billiard room was reputed to be haunted, and many times in the past, people have claimed to have heard the sound of billiard balls clicking together, coming from the empty billiard room at the dead of night. My mother tells me that she heard them many times but put it down to trains crossing Carlisle Bridge, nearly a mile away, and causing vibrations.

Finally our tour of haunted hostelries takes us to the Melling Hall Hotel near Hornby, which is haunted by a dog. A previous tenant has often heard this animal padding around the pub late at night, his collar-disc tinkling. Although he searched the pub thoroughly many times, he was never able to find where the noise came from.

So there we are, just a few of the many haunted hostelries in our county. Perhaps the next time the reader visits his favourite pub, he will look a little more carefully at that stranger standing by the corner of the bar. After all, it might only be me, but on the other hand....

5

UNEXPLAINED PHENOMENA

Despite the investigation by experts, the Church and other institutions and societies interested in paranormal phenomena, many hauntings remain a complete mystery, and any explanation as to the reasoning behind them is, at the most, inspired guesswork.

During the early 1930s a family moved into a house on Liverpool Road, Eccles. They were typical of the people living in the area at the time, in no way different from their neighbours. For two or three years, they lived quite happily, with nothing but the usual family problems and those of the difficult times to disrupt their daily lives. Then one day, after they had been in the house just over three years, they heard strange noises coming from an upstairs room and, on reaching the stairs to investigate, were quite shaken to see a dark figure, dressed in the apparel of a priest, moving downstairs towards them.

Throughout that night the noises continued, and the family were unnerved to find, on wakening the following morning, that while they were asleep, their beds had been moved to different parts of the room, unknown to the sleeping occupants. The beds were hurriedly moved to a different part of the house, but still the same thing occurred, night after night, much to the distress of the family. During the next few weeks, the priestly figure was seen quite often, usually coming down the stairs and disappearing through a wall at the bottom.

Enquiries around the neighbourhood suggested that the apparition might be that of Father Sharrock, who had been a priest at St Mary's Church and who had died in the house over thirty-five years previously. The family, themselves Roman Catholic, said prayers for the soul of the departed priest in an effort to rid the house of the apparition, but to no avail. In fact, the noises and sightings seemed to increase all the more.

In desperation the family sought help from the parish priest, the current incumbent of St Mary's, who, after listening to their story, agreed to help them. He sprinkled Holy Water and said prayers for the repose of the dead priest's soul. From that time on, the family ceased to be troubled by the noises or by the apparition, and they lived in the house peacefully for many years afterwards.

No one has been able to explain why the family should have suffered in this way, as Father Sharrock had always been a good friend to his flock and would have harmed none of them. Why previous tenants had not been bothered, why this family should have been the focus of attention, remains a mystery.

The old Lancastrians had a name for fairies and hobgoblins: 'boggart'. For mischievous elves and other bogeymen, they coined the word 'hob'. In the area around Lake Burwain at Foulridge, there are many 'fairy rings' and frequent stories of dogs, horses and cattle showing signs of fear for no apparent reason.

Not far from Lake Burwain, which is in fact a local reservoir, stands an eighteenth-century farmhouse called 'Hobstones'. Many years ago the farm area was thought by many to be the home of fairies, and there is said to be an ancient burial-ground somewhere on the land.

Some time in the late 1950s the occupant of the old farmhouse was sitting contemplating the state of the world from the comfort of his outside toilet, when the door suddenly opened and he saw a figure of a little dwarfish man, dressed as a monk, with a weather-beaten and twisted face, hold out a bleeding arm from which the lower part had been severed just below the elbow.

As this took place in broad daylight, the poor man was so startled he just stared open-mouthed at the motionless figure for several minutes, until it suddenly disappeared, as if into thin air. Nothing else happened for several weeks, and the farmer decided that someone must have been playing a joke on him – when he found out who, he would take it out of their backsides. Then suddenly, out of the blue, the figure appeared again, this time in front of the astonished farmer and his wife. It stood staring at them for several seconds before moving towards the terrified couple. When it was about an arm's length away, it disappeared again.

From that day on, the ghostly little man and his horrible wound appeared more frequently, both in the house and out on the surrounding land. As a result of this and other events, the couple shortly afterwards left the farm.

A colleague of mine knows the present occupiers of 'Hobstones' and tells me that they have never seen or heard anything during the time they have lived there.

Many of the older residents of the Gannow Lane area of Burnley will remember the baker's shop that stood there for many years, which was run by Jean and Clifford Howarth. When quite a number of the houses round about were pulled down, Jean and Clifford decided to close the shop, and between them, they converted it into a cosy little home.

About fourteen or fifteen years ago, there lived a few doors away from the shop a man in his middle fifties who was known throughout the neighbourhood as 'Old Horace'. In his younger days he had been a coal-miner, but as a result of disseminated sclerosis, he had been out of work for many years. Although he had difficulty making his way to the shop, with the aid of his stick he would tap his way down the yard to the back door and spend many hours sitting in the corner of the bakehouse, talking to Clifford.

One of his habits was to come down the yard with his dog, every Friday night, to purchase his cigarettes for the weekend, always saying to his dog as he opened the gate, "Come on, be sharp wi' thi'." One night, as a result of depression, Horace committed suicide by gassing himself, and his wife found him when she returned from the mill a few hours later.

It was on a Friday night about two weeks later, when Clifford and Jean were clearing up the bakehouse at about eight o'clock, that they heard the back gate open and the sound of a walking-stick tapping against the stone yard as footsteps shuffled to the back door. A voice was heard to say, as if to a dog, "Come on, be sharp wi' thi." Jean, without thinking, said, "Old Horace is here for his cigarettes" and went to open the door. It was only after she had opened it to find an empty yard that she realized that Horace had been dead for a fortnight.

Another, similar incident which concerned the death of a customer, occurred a year or two after this. On the opposite side of the road lived a woman in her forties who suffered from leukemia, from which she subsequently died, rather suddenly. Not only had she been a regular customer at the shop, she had also been a friend of the family, and they were used to her walking into the house at all times of day or night.

One Saturday afternoon, after the shop had closed for the weekend, Jean was getting changed in the bedroom, and Clifford was busy in the cellar, when the sound of footsteps was heard coming down the yard. Clifford heard the back door open and close and footsteps crossing the floor of the living-room, overhead. He recognized the walk as the neighbour's, because she had been lame and had her own peculiar walk. The footsteps stopped at the foot of the stairs, and they both heard a woman's voice shout, "Jean!" Again, without thinking, Jean said to herself, "Oh, Mary's come." Both Clifford and Jean then heard the footsteps retrace their way out through the back door and out of the gate. Jean hurried down the stairs and went to the back door to investigate. She found the door still locked and bolted. However, the sound was so real that it had been heard by Jean and Clifford while they had been in separate parts of the house, and neither of them has any doubt at all that they had been visited by their dead neighbour.

Neither the ghost of Horace nor that of Mary has bothered them since, and neither Jean or Clifford can account for the reasons why their customers should return from the grave.

Susan Lord and her sister were brought up in the small hamlet of Grane, which is situated on the moors between Haslingden and Blackburn.

Our story goes back to the year 1938, when the small cottage where Susan lived had changed little since being built, well over a century before. The sanitation was poor; there was no hot water and no electricity, and though gas had been installed downstairs, upstairs there was no lighting at all, save from candles.

Susan and her elder sister shared a bed in a room at the top of the stairs, under the eaves, which in those days were not underdrawn. There was no door to the bedroom, the stairs coming more or less into the room itself.

One particular evening, the two girls had gone to bed, and, as was the custom, their mother came up several minutes later to say goodnight. The girls had taken a candle to undress by, and mother, on saying goodnight, would take the candle downstairs in the interest of safety.

Susan told me, "As my mother left the room, both my sister and I saw what appeared to be a misty figure behind her. It was a classical, wraith-like thing, which seemed to follow mother down the stairs." If their mother felt anything, she certainly did not show it, but both Susan and her sister, without saying a word, retreated under the bedclothes, shaking with fright.

Looking back on it, after all these years, Susan wondered if it might have been a trick of light caused by the flickering candle, but she agrees that, if it was, then it is doubtful if both girls would have seen it at the same time and would both have been so frightened. To this day, neither Susan nor her sister has been able to explain the incident. No one ever saw this apparition again while they lived there.

During the summer of 1977 I managed to find the cottage. It had been altered and modernized beyond the recognition of its earlier tenants. An attractive young woman answered the door and, in answer to my questions, said that neither she nor her husband had any inkling of a ghost and that they did not really believe in such things anyway. She did say, however, that there was sometimes a funny smell up the stairs and the cat would never go up there!

During a performance, there is a definite air of magic in an old theatre, but once the audience has gone home and only the working lights are on, the auditorium becomes a pretty eerie place. When a theatre is rumoured to be haunted, the atmosphere late at night can be quite frightening.

An acquaintance of mine (I will call him Fred) was a night-watchman at the Grand Theatre, Lancaster, several years ago. He had heard that the old place was said to be haunted by the ghost of the eighteenth-century actress Sarah Siddons, but being a practical, down-to-earth sort of chap, he had shrugged off any fears he might have had. After all, he was disabled and needed a job.

He was a well-built man and in his day had been able to handle himself: he had been afraid of neither man nor beast. Now, as a disabled ex-merchant seaman, he had had to take on this job as watchman, a job he had held for about two years. In this time he had seen nothing but the odd rat, certainly no ghost of Sarah Siddons, or of anyone else for that matter.

Each night, having checked the doors and done his fire-round, he would sit for a while in his room to eat his supper. He had done this nearly every night for the past two years, at about the same time each night. One particular night, the working lights were still on, as one of the stage electricians was working late, somewhere back-stage, so Fred decided to sit in the auditorium to eat his supper.

He told me: "I remember it as if it were yesterday. I sat in either row E or F, in the end seat, near the centre aisle. Suddenly, I sensed that someone was walking down the centre aisle and, thinking it was the electrician, turned to ask him if he wanted a brew of tea." To his surprise, Fred saw the figure of an elderly woman seemingly floating down the aisle towards him. She appeared to be cut off, just above the ankles, and she had a smile on her face. Gliding past the row of seats where he sat, she disappeared through a door at the far end of the theatre, near the stage.

Over the years, other members of staff have seen her, as have touring theatricals. Fred saw her once more before he retired, but, to my knowledge, no one has seen her in recent years. Perhaps her reason for being there is no more. No one knows why she haunted the old theatre, but I would venture to suggest that she just loved the old place.

The country lanes around Longridge were once said to be haunted by a mysterious and evil ghost, known locally as 'the headless woman'. From behind she looked normal enough, an old lady hobbling along in her shawl and bonnet, carrying a basket under one arm. She would walk quietly beside anyone who tried to pass her and would listen politely to their conversation. Suddenly, when they least expected it, she would turn towards the unfortunate victim, revealing that the inside of her bonnet contained – nothing. As they recoiled in terror, the old woman would lift the cloth from the top of her basket, and out would spring the head, shrieking with laughter and snapping viciously. The head would then chase the hapless victim for several miles, bounding along the road behind him.

One night the local drunk encountered her, as he made his way back home after a drinking session at Clitheroe. The sight of the ghost soon sobered him up, and he raced across the fields to the safety of his own home. His wife showed little sympathy for the poor man, who arrived home in a state of abject terror. She just said, "If it makes thi fain o'thi own hearthstooan, I'll be glad on it, for it's more than a woman wi' a heead on her shoulders has bin able t'do!"

Several incidents occurred some years ago at Kempnough Hall, Worsley, which is said to have had associations with the Tudor 'magician' John Dee, who appears to have left some of his evil influences on the old hall. Sam Derbyshire, a tenant, went berserk one night, killed his wife with an axe, cut his young son's throat and finally shot himself. No satisfactory reason was ever given as to why he should have done this.

People have refused even to enter the hall on occasion because of the sinister atmosphere that would envelop the place at times. I heard of two children, some years ago, who came down from their bedroom one night and complained that their bed was full of pins. (Remnants of witchcraft perhaps?)

One lady told me the following story which happened to her several years ago, when she stayed at the hall, with her grandmother, who had lived there for a good number of years. One evening, towards the end of the grandmother's life, the grand-daughter was quietly sewing, when suddenly grannie asked her what would she like her to leave for her in her Will. The grand-daughter told me: "I had noticed on several visits a beautiful crucifix above grannie's bed, so I asked her if she would leave that to me. Grannie looked mystified and said that she did not have a crucifix above her bed." The grand-daughter argued with the old woman that she had seen it many times, so grannie told her to go and have another look. Needless to say, there was no sign of a crucifix.

Some months later, a young child staying at the hall went up to fetch something for grannie from her room. She was gone for a very long time and, on her return downstairs, was asked what had taken her so long. The child replied that she had been into grannie's bedroom and was standing watching the beautiful angel kneeling on the bed, saying her prayers.

Both these events remained unexplained; grannie is long dead; but the two ladies who had these experiences are still very much alive and remember the incidents as if they had happened only yesterday.

About four years ago, while visiting Carr House at Bretherton, my wife and I had rather an unnerving experience which has remained unexplained.

Carr House was built in 1613 by Thomas Stones of London and Andrew Stones of Amsterdam, for their brother John, a sheep-farmer in the district. The building is worth inspection on its own merit, being probably one of the oldest in this part of Lancashire and still retaining the scars of the window-tax of 1695.

It was in this house, in a room over the entrance porch, that one Jeremiah Horrocks, a local clergyman, calculated the time and day, in the winter of 1639, when the planet Venus would be seen in transit across the face of the sun.

For many years the house stood empty, an abject and desolate ruin, but demolition was opposed by public outcry and eventually it was bought by public subscription and in 1965 put at the disposal of the late Barry Elder and his wife, for use as a doll museum. It was soon transformed from an empty ruin into a fairy-tale home for dolls from all over the world. Time past, present and future seemed to be caught up and held motionless.

The brochure available at the museum made no mention of the building's being haunted, except to say, "There is, of course, just an uneasy feeling that the dolls might perhaps come alive at night when the oil-lamps are lit and the last visitors have departed reluctantly to their own homes, though few of them would care to sleep here at night, it seems."

My wife and I last visited the museum in 1975. We had been fascinated by the exhibition on the ground floor, where, in the main entrance, the inglenooks beside the large open fireplace were occupied by tall, dignified dolls, sitting on high-backed wing chairs, with doll 'children' on their laps. In the centre of the oak-beamed hall, old grandmother dolls sat, peering through spectacles at the laden tea-table.

We climbed the cage newell staircase (which, it is thought, has only one other counterpart of the period existing in this country) and continued to the top floor. Crossing to the room farthest from the stairs, we entered a small area under the eaves. Here I was conscious of a terrible feeling of evil and fear. My wife said later that on our first visit to the house she had felt this sensation but had never mentioned it. However, on this visit in 1975, we both felt the 'presence' surrounding us, rather like a blanket of evil, enveloping the area in which we stood. It was nothing but a feeling, albeit frightening, and it was remarkable because it was localized. Move away a few feet and the feeling ended; move back to the spot again and it returned.

I wrote to Mrs Elder, asking if she or her husband had ever experienced something similar, while they occupied the house. In her reply to me, Mrs Elder said that other people had mentioned similar reactions to an atmosphere in this area, but that she herself had never had any feelings of foreboding or evil. She went on to say: "On the contrary, as far as I can gather, Carr House had always been tenanted by farmers, who are usually concerned with earthly matters. However, we are not to know what went on in the days of religious persecution." Here, possibly, lies a clue to the atmosphere of the house.

There has been some architectural change in this part of the house – the evidence is there to see, quite plainly, and this is the area where these sensations are strongest. It is known that there was a bolt-hole on this floor at some time in the past. Neither Mrs Elder nor anyone else, so far as I can ascertain, has seen or heard anything, but several people have felt this atmosphere. Nothing much seems to be known about previous tenants, nor can anyone throw any light on any occurrence which would justify any hauntings.

It is just possible that a priest was found and killed here during the Reformation, or, alternatively, that when Lord Derby was soundly beaten by Cromwell at Wigan in 1648, one of his volunteers, making his way back to his home in Scotland, was given refuge here and was either discovered and killed or, what is even more likely, starved to death behind some secret panel. It has not been possible to discover whether or not a skeleton was ever found here. Could it be that there is still a secret panel waiting to be discovered, complete with skeleton, in this area?

The house now stands empty again, alas, and to date it has not been possible for me to do any further investigation, but some day, when new tenants take over, I would be interested in going back to see whether or not that atmosphere is still there.

In the early 1950s a young couple underwent a terrifying ordeal in their small terraced house in Chorley – an ordeal which they will have difficulty in forgetting. They had been married for about two years, and, this being their first home, they had put quite a lot of money into decoration and improvements. It would appear that these alterations to the property were, to some extent, responsible for the troubles which were to follow, but, as the house had no previous record of hauntings, the affair remained a mystery.

One day, the slight grey outline of a small man suddenly materialized beside the fireplace. From that day on, the figure appeared quite regularly and was usually accompanied by the sound of what seemed to be the scratching of a dog against the stone floor. Most frightening of all, though, were the low moaning sounds which seemed to come from upstairs and which rose to a weird and horrifying scream.

Footsteps could be heard crossing the floor of the rooms upstairs and then making their way down the stairs. On investigation, nothing was ever found.

The effect on the nerves of the young couple, after several weeks of this, can well be imagined, particularly as they had enlisted the aid of the local priest and, despite his blessing the house and sprinkling Holy Water, the desired effect had not been reached. The fearful ghost simply refused to budge.

A short while afterwards, the young couple asked a relative to baby-sit for them, while they went out for a couple of hours. On their return home, they found the poor baby-sitter in a state of terror as a result of what had happened while they were out. Sitting alone with the baby and the dog, listening to the radio, she had suddenly heard footsteps overhead, which eventually began to descend the stairs. Thinking it was an intruder, she sent the dog to seek him out. The dog dashed out of the room, only to rush back again seconds later and cower, yelping, under a chair, where it remained, shaking with fright, for some time. On hearing the distraught girl's story, the young couple went upstairs to see what had been going on. They were shocked to find that their bed had been stripped, bedding was scattered all over the room, and the whole place looked as if it had been ransacked.

The youngsters had now had enough and, within a matter of days, moved out to stay with relatives. Whether or not succeeding occupants have had any similar experiences, I have been unable to find out, but the couple, now approaching middle age, still remember the incidents. They are hardly likely to forget.

Finally, here is an unexplained phenomenon which, although it does

Colne Hall. Once a manor house, now part of the Co-operative complex, it is haunted by the ghost of a pathetic Victorian child.

Burnley Central Library. A phantom pianist is said to haunt the lecture theatre to the left of the main entrance on the first floor.

Two haunted pubs – *Below left:* 'Smackwater Jack's', Burnley, with a warehouse-labourer's ghost in its wine-bar. *Below right:* The Stork Hotel, Billinge, once a prison, now haunted by a rowdy Cavalier.

not involve a spectre, is none the less fascinating.

There are many recorded instances of totally mysterious manifestations of liquids which appear from nowhere. Early in 1873, Bank House at Eccleston, near Chorley, was the scene of one of these so-called 'poltergeist flows': water is said to have rained down on one of the rooms, ruining the furnishings and soaking the inhabitants. However, investigation proved the ceilings to be quite dry. Everyone who investigated the phenonemon was of the opinion that it was genuine and that there was no question of imposture. The source and reason behind this particular phenonemon remains a mystery to this day.

Similarly, a mysterious phenomenon was reported in 1919, when a field of wheat appeared overnight. In the previous year, when a drought had killed off a field of wheat at Ormskirk, the farmer did not bother to re-seed it to give a wheat yield the following year. However, in August 1919, one of the best crops of vigorous young wheat ever seen in the area suddenly appeared overnight. The phenomenon has been repeated in various parts of the world. Wheat-seed has been recorded as having 'fallen from the sky', but no explanation has been offered. Fish, frogs and organic matter have also been recorded as falling from the sky in various parts of the world.

6

HEALING SPIRITS

Most older hospitals have a resident ghost, usually a grey lady or a nun, and Lancashire's hospitals are no exception. Because of the many life-and-death dramas played out daily in our hospitals, it is a wonder more ghosts have not been reported. Understandably the authorities will not admit to their hospitals having a ghost, healing spirit or otherwise, but they do exist, and many have been seen by both staff and patients.

A young nurse at Sharoe Green hospital, Preston, was tending a patient at the bedside when she was overcome by a feeling of intense coldness and the feeling of someone, or something, dragging at her legs. From the corner of her eye, she caught a fleeting glimpse of a figure disappearing out of the ward. She noticed that it wore what appeared to be a pointed hat, rather like the pointed hat usually associated with witches.

Puzzled, she finished tending her patient and forgot about the incident until later in the day, when she happened to mention it to her colleagues. She learned that this was the ghost of a psychiatric patient who always wore a pointed hat, a gift from a relative. She had stuffed it solid with paper and other materials and, using it as a base upon which to stand, had hanged herself. Her ghost was seen frequently by staff and patients alike.

Though what follows is not a ghost story in the true sense, St John of God's Hospital, Silverdale, was the setting of a paranormal experience.

A correspondent of mine, visiting her husband who was lying gravely ill, his life in the balance, suddenly she smelled the unmistakable scent of roses, which was so overpowering that she mentioned it to one of the Brothers who ran the hospital. He replied that he too could smell them, and my correspondent was not to worry, because it was St Theresa who had come in answer to her prayers. St Theresa was caring for her husband, he said, and now he knew that the patient would pull through. Sure enough, not long afterwards, the husband began to pick up and eventually got better. While researching for this book, I met this gentleman and can confirm that he has made a wonderful recovery from a very severe stroke.

One does not normally associate maternity hospitals with the dead, as this is where life begins – however, one fairly modern maternity unit in north-east Lancashire boasts a tragic ghost, which has been seen more than once in the last five years.

In January 1971, Margaret Smith, a nursing auxiliary at the maternity unit attached to this hospital, was working night duty. A mother had given birth to a child a short time before, and Margaret was cleaning out the delivery room. It was about 2 am. Behind her, the wide doors were fastened open, and, as she bent over the bed to change the rubber sheet, she caught sight of a figure dressed in white and wearing a nurse's cap, going down the corridor. Margaret said: "She was wearing a nurse's uniform, but nothing like the uniform worn at this hospital, which was blue." The figure seemed to glide along the corridor and appeared to have no feet. There was no sound, but that in itself is not unusual for nursing staff, although Margaret considered it odd that a strange nurse should be on this floor. "There were no other mums-to-be awaiting delivery, and all the staff were on the ward, which was upstairs," she continued.

Finishing her work, Margaret asked her colleagues who it was had come downstairs and was even more mystified when she was informed that no one had left the floor. Someone then said, "Did you know we had a ghost?" Apparently, it is that of a nurse from another hospital, who died in this unit during childbirth just after it opened, and whose sad ghost still roams the corridors from time to time.

A certain major hospital in Liverpool has a number of ghosts which have been seen over two dozen times, by both staff and patients.

In the early hours of one morning, about eight years ago, a nursing sister and two of her nurses saw a strange movement of something with no particular shape, at the top of the ward. They had heard that the ward was haunted by the ghost of a patient who had died there many years before. The three nurses watched 'it' for several minutes, then one of the nurses said that she did not believe in ghosts and would go and see just what it was.

She began to walk up the ward but, after a few paces, stopped, saying that something was preventing her moving any further. The nursing sister, deciding to see for herself, was also unable to pass through this invisible barrier. A few minutes later the 'figure' melted into thin air.

The maternity section of this same hospital also has a ghost, which has been seen by members of the staff and has been recognized as that of a staff sister who died some years ago. One nurse claims to have actually spoken to the figure and that it replied, saying it wished to look after the babies and patients. Some mothers have refused to have their babies in this ward after experiencing paranormal phenomena.

Yet a third ghost haunts the X-Ray department. This was originally a ward which had been converted and is not used at night because of an apparition which still appears.

Manchester's Crumpsall Hospital has a ghost on one ward, which has a passion for plastic bowls, bed-pans and lavatory-chains. Staff and patients have been disturbed by the rattling of lavatory-chains and the banging of lavatory-seats. When staff have gone to investigate, they have found the toilets empty, but the chains have been swinging mysteriously. Plastic bowls and bed-pans have been seen flying across the sluice-room accompanied by chilling feelings, and on one occasion a vague figure was seen by a nursing sister standing by the television set. No one knows the origin of this particular ghost.

The David Lewis Northern Hospital at Liverpool has a ghost which is associated with the sea. This is the ghost of a smuggler who was intercepted by the Customs and Excise men while running his illicit cargo ashore at Wallasey. As he rowed hard to escape, his boat was washed by a heavy tide until it eventually sank under him and he was forced to swim to the shore. Staggering ashore, he collapsed, and the waiting Customs officers began to kick and beat him as he lay on the beach, until he shortly died of his injuries.

This all happened within sight and sound of where the hospital was later built. Today, from time to time, the ghost of the smuggler can be seen, prowling along the hospital corridors, dressed in the costume of a sailor of the eighteenth century.

The site on which the Royal Southern Hospital now stands is said to be haunted by the restless spirits of African slaves, who, during the great slaving days of Liverpool, were confined to cells in this part of the city, prior to being shipped to the plantations of the West Indies and the Deep South of North America. Many unfortunate slaves died here from suffocation, hunger, disease and, very often, violence.

Still in Liverpool, the nurses' home of the Liverpool Royal Infirmary, built on the site of a big old house in Pembroke Place, was the scene of a tragic accident: many years ago, a young bride, still in her wedding-gown, fell to her death from an upstairs window. Downstairs, the wedding guests continued with the reception, unaware of the tragedy that had taken place. The ghost of the sad bride has been seen in the nurses' home, wearing her white gown and veiled head-dress, a tragic reminder of that happy day which turned to sadness, many years ago.

Some years ago there was a mining disaster at one of the collieries near Burnley, and the victims, both injured and dying, were taken to the Victoria Hospital in Burnley. It appears that most of the wards were full and so several of the victims were left on stretchers and trolleys in the corridors until room could be found for them in the wards. Some of the miners died during this time, and it is thought to be one of these victims whose ghost is seen from time to time, aimlessly roaming the hospital corridors.

As Stockport has now become a part of Greater Manchester, the ghost that haunts St Thomas's Hospital can be recorded here. For years there have been stories told of a ghostly white lady who appears only at night and always in the same place. She is described as being a kindly, smiling lady who wears a novice's habit, or possibly the white robes of a nurse. She is said to hover above the ground and is surrounded by an intense light. Who the white lady is, no one knows, but most people are agreed that her appearances are usually the prelude to a death.

7

SCREAMING SKULLS

With a grisly nostalgia that we mortals cannot understand, some ghosts stubbornly cling to their mortal earthly remains. There are several country houses which list among their varied attractions the skull of a former member of the family. If these skulls are removed, or if any attempt is made to bury them, then all hell is let loose around the house. Hideous screams carry from room to room; thunder and lightning are called down upon the culprits, and dire misfortune falls upon the occupants. No wonder few care to put the matter to the test.

Browsholme Hall, the home of the Parker family, has one such skull, believed to be that of one who was martyred after the Pilgrimage of Grace. When the top storey of the house was removed in 1703, the skull was brought down to the family chapel. It was always treated with respect and reverence, but in the 1850s Edward Parker, then a boy, buried it in the garden as a practical joke. Disaster followed disaster: the façade began to fall away from the Tudor walls; fires broke out under mysterious circumstances, and there were many deaths in the family.

Finally the frightened boy confessed, and the skull was dug up and returned to its cupboard. Everything returned to normal, but the family had to move out until the house was again made habitable.

At Appley Bridge, near Wigan, there stands a rather strange house, known as 'Skull House', riddled with mysterious cupboards, leaded windows decorated with skulls, very low ceilings with thick, skull-cracking beams, boarded-up cellars and various odd nooks and crannies, including a priests' hide.

On a beam in the living-room rests a discoloured human skull, which is said to bring bad luck and unwelcome screams and other disturbances, if it is taken out of the house. No one knows who was the original owner of the skull, but it has been at Skull House for as long as people can remember, and there are a number of theories surrounding its identity. Some people believe it to be the skull of a monk, who, while being pursued by Cromwell's troops, climbed up the wide chimney to hide in a small room above. Legend has it that the Roundheads, knowing of his attempt to hide, lit a huge fire in the grate, and that it was not very long before the poor cleric was forced to surrender. It is said that the monk was then beheaded and that it is his skull that rests on the beam, while his body is buried elsewhere in the house.

Another theory is that the skull is that of a knight who lived in the days of King Arthur. The story goes that a fierce battle was fought on the banks of the River Douglas and that this skull was found there many years after the event. Medical evidence, however, adds further intrigue by suggesting that the skull may have belonged to a woman.

Whoever it does belong to is determined that the skull should remain at the house, for it is said that ill-fortune will follow anyone who takes it away, and anyway, legend says that even when the skull was once thrown into the river, it somehow managed to find its way back into the house.

Wardley Hall, near Swinton, has a resident skull preserved in a niche in the wall of the staircase. Over the past two hundred years, some weird tales have been told surrounding this relic.

Tradition tells us that this is the skull of Roger Downes, the last male heir of the Downes family, who was an abandoned courtier of Charles II. While in London on a drunken frolic, he vowed to his companions that he would kill the first person he met and, drawing his sword, staggered along until he met his victim, a poor tailor, whom he ran through with his weapon and killed on the spot. Downes was arrested for the crime, but his involvement with the royal Court procured him a pardon.

Soon after this, he is alleged to have been involved in a riot on London Bridge, when a watchman struck him with the 'bill' which they all carried and severed his head from his shoulders. The body was thrown over the parapet into the Thames, but his head was rescued by his friends and was carefully packed and returned to his sisters at Wardley. His sister Maria opened the package and read of her brother's fate from a note which was enclosed.

For many years, the bleached skull at the Hall was said to have been that of Roger Downes, but towards the end of the eighteenth century this theory was disproved.

Round about the year 1780, the Downes family vault in Wigan church was opened up and a coffin was discovered, which had on it an inscription to the memory of Roger Downes. The coffin was opened, and the skeleton, complete with head, was found intact. Whatever had been the cause of death, the upper part of the skull had been sawn off, a little above the eyes. It was obviously the work of a surgeon, perhaps in an attempt at an early post-mortem.

However, to return to the skull. The bone of the lower jaw has become detached, and there are signs of violence to it. Apparently, at some time in the past it was been broken up, in an attempt to rid the Hall of the weird happenings.

There is another theory attached to the skull, which is more likely to be nearer the truth which, like many other skull-stories, relates back to the days of Roman Catholic persecution.

The Hall was purchased by the Downes family in about 1600 and until 1640, Francis Downes often sheltered his old friend Edward Barlow, a staunch Catholic priest. (Names differ here; some opinion states that it was Ambrose Barlow, a Benedictine monk.) During the Easter of 1640-41, Barlow was seized by a Protestant mob, led by the vicar of Leigh, and hauled off to a magistrate at Winwick. While being held in custody he apparently suffered a stroke, but this did not prevent him being hauled off to Lancaster Castle, where he was held for four months, pending his trial and subsequent conviction. At the age of fifty-four, he was executed at Lancaster Moor, surrounded by a large crowd, which included Francis Downes and some of his friends.

Downes rescued the priest's head and took it for safe keeping to Wardley Hall.

For a good many years the skull was kept on view at the head of the staircase, and whichever theory is correct, it is a known fact that any attempt to remove it for burial brings repercussions in the form of violent storms and other disturbances. In the past, the skull has been burned, cut to pieces and thrown into the river, but it has always, somehow, managed to return to the Hall.

The real identity of the skull is probably that of Father Barlow, and the story of Downes was possibly put about to hide the identity, at a time when Catholics were hounded unmercifully.

The Manor at Turton, north of Bolton, is said to have been granted by William the Conqueror to one de Orell, for services rendered during the conquest of 1066. De Orell erected a strong house for defence, which was afterwards known as 'Turton Tower'. It is said that the wages of the workmen were then only one penny a day, but despite this, the Tower was built in such magnificent style that the family never recovered from financial difficulties.

From the early thirteenth century, the Lathoms held the Manor, passing it once more to the Orells, descendants of the original builder, in 1420.

By tradition, the Tower is haunted by a lady who can occasionally be heard passing along the corridors and into rooms, sounding as if she is dressed in very stiff, rustling silk. I believe the sound is very distinct as she sweeps along the broad massive oak staircase, which leads from the main hall into the upper rooms. She has also been seen, a lady in black, ascending the stairs leading to the top floor of the Tower and is said to glide across an upstairs room where it seems as if she jumps down an old garderobe shaft, which leads into the old original drainage system and which could, in the old days, have been a means of escape, for she no doubt dates back to the persecution and the Orells, and is most probably in some way connected with illegal priestly activities.

Recently, a wooden cradle was seen being rocked by invisible hands, and there are reports of mysterious bangings, screechings and knockings, which, it is thought, may be connected with the Timberbottom Skulls now kept in a glass case in the Tower.

A short distance from Turton Tower used to stand a farmhouse, by the name of 'Timberbottom', or 'Skull House', so called becuase of the two skulls which were originally kept here. One appears to be the skull of a female, the other of a male, and they were fished out of Bradshaw Brook at Turton around 1751. On examination it will be seen that one of the skulls is badly decayed, and the other appears to have been cut through by a blow from some sharp instrument.

Apparently, these two skulls used to rest on the mantleshelf at Timberbottom, and whenever they were moved, all sorts of mysterious activities commenced. Bangings, thumpings, screechings and ghostly visitations drove the tenants near to insanity. They threw the skulls in the river but were forced to recover them because of the disturbances that followed. The skulls are said to have been buried several times at Bradshaw Chapel, but even then they had to be exhumed and taken back. Eventually, they found their way to Bradshaw Hall and finally to Turton Tower, where they remain to this day, but by all accounts they will not remain silent for long.

Who do the skulls belong to? Again we can only look to folk-lore. In 1882 it was said that they had been obtained by an old woman who claimed that they were the skulls of two robbers, and the following story was told.

Apparently, late in the seventeenth century, the family of the house had been away and the house was left in the care of a manservant. One night, a gang of mounted robbers came to the house, and one of them tried to gain entrance through the window of the cheese-room. The faithful servant seized hold of a sword and severed the head from the robber. A second member of the gang received the same rough justice. The headless bodies fell to the ground, where they were picked up by the remaining members of the gang, who made off leaving a trail of blood and the severed heads behind them.

In due course, it was discovered that one of the heads was female, so the story was changed, and modern versions say that the skulls belong to a farmer and his wife. The farmer is said to have murdered his wife and then committed suicide. Personally, I prefer the first version.

8

GHOSTLY DAMES

Apart from Mother Demdike, Old Chattox and Alice Nutter of Pendle, the three best-known old women in the folk-history of Lancashire were Dame Sykes, Miss Beswick of Birchen Bower and Marjory Hilton, the Fylde witch. Legend and fact have combined to make them as much a part of Lancashire life as their notorious Pendle sisters.

Like the Pendle witches, they were real people whose lives are now clouded in a mixture of fact and fiction but who, even today, let it be known that they are still with us, at least in spirit.

Marjory Hilton of Catforth was found dead, crushed between a barrel and a wall, and was buried by torchlight on 2nd May 1705, beside the path in St Anne's churchyard, Woodplumpton.

Old Meg, as she was known, was a crafty old girl, who was able to turn herself into innocent items of domestic equipment, which was supposed to explain why she was never caught red-handed when she was up to her tricks. Despite her reputation for cleverness, she lived a frugal life, existing mainly on a diet of seasoned boiled groats and stolen milk, in her hovel of a cottage near Wesham. A number of legends have grown around her, and stories of her crafty wiles are still told among the older people of the Fylde, as they have been for generation after generation, providing our ancestors with an escape from their dismal and humdrum lives and satisfying their basic human need for a story.

My favourite story about Meg tells of a cottage becoming vacant at Catforth on which she set her sights and in which entered into a strange bargain with the landlord. She said that she would turn herself into a hare, the landlord would unloosen his dogs, with the exception of his notorious big black hound, and if she gave them the slip and reached the cottage in safety, it would be hers. The landlord agreed to the wager, and Meg, turning into a hare, bolted away, the dogs behind her quickly outpaced.

The landlord, as big a rogue as Meg, could not resist the temptation of loosing the black hound from its leash, and it streaked off in pursuit, soon overtaking the other dogs and catching up with the hare at the door of the witch's cottages, nipping it on the heel.

Old Meg got her cottage but after that had a limp which was to remain with her for the rest of her life.

This is just one of the legends which surrounded her when she was alive, but even after her death she refused to lay quiet. She is said to have scratched her way to the top of the grave so often that the priest had to exorcize her. Eventually she was re-interred, head downwards under a large boulder-stone, where she remains to this day. But is she at rest?

One elderly lady told me that, as a child, she spent a lot of time with her grandparents who were farmers at Woodplumpton. She said that one day grandfather came home and said that Major Lingard, a neighbouring farmer, had seen Old Meg in the lane by 'The Running Pump', the local pub. The major swore that he and others, quite reputable people, had seen her on many occasions. She told me that one day someone, on seeing Meg's ghost, hit out at her with a broom, at which she disappeared, but several minutes later a hare was seen limping across a nearby field, with a patch of fur torn out of its head!

One amusing tale associated with Woodplumpton Church and old Meg is of a funeral which took place there at the beginning of this century. It seems that the deceased had been rather a tall person, well over six feet, and that his coffin, being, as it were, made to measure, was over the regulation length and therefore would not fit into the ready-dug grave. To the absolute horror of all the good mourners assembled, the sexton, who was renowned for his outspoken impatience, said, "Shove t'bugger in end up, same as they did wi' Old Meg and stand 'im on 'is 'ead!"

Whether that was true or not I don't know, but not so many years ago, when a family party visited Woodplumpton Church, an incident occurred which at least one member of the party will always remember.

A small boy who was a member of the party wandered alone into the church, while the remainder were looking around the graveyard.

He soon came running out again, very frightened and distressed. When asked the cause of his fright, he replied that nothing would make him go back into the church again, as he had been chased around the inside by a wicked old woman, dressed in old-fashioned clothes.

It would appear that even after 250 years or more, Old Meg is still up to her mischief. Even today in Woodplumpton, among some of the farmers, whenever anything goes wrong on a farm, from the cream going sour to the death of a calf or piglet, it is still considered to be the work of Old Meg, and many a naughty child is still threatened with a swipe across the backside from Old Meg's broomstick.

Slightly more up to date is the story associated with Hannah Beswick, a well-to-do landowner who, during the middle of the eighteenth century, lived on the outskirts of Manchester. When, in 1745, Bonnie Prince Charlie invaded England and advanced south into Lancashire, she deemed it wise to hide her money and valuables, and they remained hidden until her death in 1768.

In those days, many people had a terrible dread of being buried alive, and Miss Beswick was no exception. It was understandable in her case, as one of her brothers, while in a state of trance, was believed to have died, only to be taken from his coffin some time later, after having begun to recover and show signs of life. Because of this fear, Miss Beswick left her house, Birchen Bower, to a young doctor, Charles White, with the unusual stipulation that she should not be buried but that her body should be embalmed and kept above ground. Every twenty-one years the embalmed body should be taken back to the house and left in the granary for seven days.

To comply with the Will, Miss Beswick's body was coated with tar and wrapped in heavy bandages. Her face, however, was left uncovered.

Now, one would have thought that, with the fulfilment of these last requests, Miss Beswick would have rested in peace, but that was not to be: on many occasions her ghost was to be seen wandering around her old home, dressed as she had been in life, in a black gown and white lace cap, usually passing between the old barn and the pond. Often, it was said, the old barn glowed as if on fire.

For many years, Dr White kept the enbalmed body at his own home, Sale Priory, but eventually, on his death, it was moved to the museum of the Manchester Natural History Society, where it became an object of popular interest.

One hundred years after Miss Beswick's death, the Commissioners of the Society, charged with the re-arrangement of the collection, in their wisdom considered the retention of the 'mummy' no longer desirable and made arrangements for it to be given a decent Christian burial. So finally old Miss Beswick was laid to rest at Harperhay cemetery on 22nd July 1868.

Meanwhile, a number of alterations were being made to Birchen Bower. It was renovated, after being empty for some years, and converted into a number of small houses to be rented by handloom weavers and labourers. However, Miss Beswick's ghost was often heard in the house and was seen, on occasions, to disappear at a particular spot, a flagstone in the parlour of one wing, which was occupied by Joe of Tamers, a poor handloom weaver.

One day, Joe was pulling up part of the flagstone floor, to enable him to erect a loom, when he came across a hoard of gold wedges, which were worth about three pounds in those days. These wedges are on record as having been converted into currency at Oliphants of Manchester.

After this, Miss Beswick's restless spirit was seen quite often, her attitude seeming to be one of defiance, streams of blue light darting from her eyes, her entire attitude one of anger and menace. Often, on moonlit nights, her headless figure was seen near the pond, giving rise to speculation that more of her wealth was hidden thereabouts. Strange, unearthly sounds would be heard coming from the barn, but investigation could prove nothing.

The hauntings continued until Birchen Bower was demolished, and even when Ferranti built their factory here, people still claimed to have seen or heard the ghost of Hannah Beswick.

Our third spirited dame can be found in a secluded spot on the banks of the Mellor Brook, not far from Samlesbury Hall. Here, many years ago, stood a lonely farmhouse which was occupied for several generations by a family named Sykes, who took their name from the homestead when the forests around the area were cleared, and from the green pastures lying a short distance from a broad and deep part of the brook; it became known as 'Sykes Lumb Farm'. The Sykes have been extinct for generations, but the doings of one of the family have provided the area with what is probably the most famous ghost story in the county.

Tradition has it that one of the last owners of the farm became very rich, partly through the constant hoarding of his ancestors, partly by the thrift of his wife and partly by the discovery of hidden treasure belonging to a former tenant.

The outbreak of the Wars of the Roses in the fifteenth century took away not only much of the wealth of Lancashire but quite a large proportion of the population too. Old Sykes and his wife had no children and since he himself was too old to be called upon to fight in the war, their only anxiety was the thought of their wealth being stolen by marauding thieves. Dame Sykes had no intention of becoming dependent on the Southworths of Samlesbury Hall or of seeking charity from the abbot of Whalley, so she decided to have her wealth hidden in a safe place. The valuables were carefully fastened in large earthenware jars and buried deep beneath the roots of an apple tree in the orchard.

Years passed, but the troubles in the country continued, until finally the Yorkists were beaten and the reins of government passed into the hands of the House of Lancaster. Peace and happiness returned to the countryside and to old Dame Sykes, for her husband had by now died, leaving her the sole possessor of their buried wealth. Her happiness was short-lived, however, for not many months later she suddenly joined her departed husband. In fact, her passing was so sudden that she had no opportunity to disclose the whereabouts of the hidden treasure. Rumour had not failed to give her credit for having amassed considerable wealth, but although her relatives searched thoroughly, they were unable to find where the jars were hidden.

Eventually the farm passed into other hands, and poor old Dame Sykes might have been forgotten if her ghost, unable to rest, had not continued to visit the farm. Sometimes, at dusk, the neighbouring peasants were met by an old wrinkled woman dressed in ancient clothes, passing along the road which crossed the Lumb. Fear, however, always prevented anyone from doing more than heading in the opposite direction. The ghost never made a sound, never lifted her head, but helped herself along noiselessly, by means of a crooked stick, which bore no resemblance to anything in use at that time. Sometimes she was seen in the old barn, at others in the house, but more often than not in the orchard, standing by an old apple tree.

Generations came and went, and still the visitations of Dame Sykes' ghost continued. One old chronicler described seeing her in her short, old-fashioned gown, striped petticoat and stick. He was so alarmed that he ran away, despite having urgent work to do. She was not there when he went to take an apple, but as soon as he raised his hand to pick the fruit, she appeared in front of him.

At last, one brave occupant of the farm, made braver no doubt by several pints of the local ale, decided to wait for the ghost to appear and question her as to the reason of her visits. She soon appeared and glided ahead of him as if she wanted him to follow. He staggered after her shouting questions, but she made no reply. After gliding towards the stump of an old apple tree, she pointed to a part of the orchard which had never been disturbed. Like a clap of thunder, the significance struck him. He woke the entire household; spades and forks were brought out, and a frenzied dig began on a large scale. The treasure was found deep down in the earth, and as the earth was being moved, the apparition was to be seen standing at the edge of the trench.

When the last jar was lifted out, an unearthly smile passed over the withered features; her form became less and less distinct and finally vanished completely. Since then the old farm has ceased to be haunted, and old Sykes' wife has hopefully found eternal rest. But, for many years after, even up until the airfield was laid on this land, there were many people who walked a little quicker past the Lumb, fearful that they might once more be confronted by the ghost of old Sykes' wife.

Whalley Abbey – the gateway, where the ghost of Abbot Paslew
has been seen and where his photograph was taken some years ago.

Smithills Hall, Bolton. The upper room on the left is where Marsh
was accused of being a heretic. To the right of the lower window,
in the passage, his footprint can be seen.

Todd Cottage, Melling, the home of Mr and Mrs J. Mulroy and
their friendly spectre, the Rev. B. Grenside.

9

PHANTOM MONKS

As I drove out to Whalley Abbey one autumn evening, I could not help wondering what I was letting myself in for. I had received an invitation to spend the night there as the guest of Mr Ian Green, the manager, to discuss some of the supernatural occurrences that are becoming more frequent at the old abbot's house. I was to spend the night alone in the part of the building where most of the activities took place.

I had not heard of any activities in the house itself, but I had been told of people who had had experiences of paranormal activity in the Abbey ruins.

A middle-aged lady told me how she had been enchanted one evening as she sat among the ruins, listening to the singing of a *Te Deum*, which appeared to be coming from the ruined nave. She assures me she was quite alone at the time.

Two students told of witnessing a ghostly procession of monks, one late summer's evening. They were astonished to see, coming from the direction of the south transept, a number of monks, heads bowed, hands together as if in prayer. They watched fascinated for several minutes, until the procession reached the ruined choir and the whole scene faded before their eyes.

The monks first came to Whalley from Stanlow, in the thirteenth century, after appropriating property which included the rectories of Eccles, Rochdale and Blackburn.

In 1289, on the death of its rector, the Pope gave the monks licence to appropriate Whalley church, but it was not until 1296 that Abbot Gregory and a small party of monks arrived from Stanlow to take possession of the rectory house and begin working on the building of the Abbey.

The last abbot of Whalley was John Paslew, who was charged with treason and executed at Lancaster in 1537, following which the Earl of Sussex was sent on the King's instructions to take possession of the Abbey, as forfeited property.

In 1553, after the dissolution of the monasteries, Whalley Abbey was bought by John Braddyll of Brockall and Richard Assheton of Lever, for the sum of £2,151 3s 9d, and between them they divided the property.

Over the years the properties were sub-divided; the abbot's house and the infirmary buildings were dismantled, and on the site of these was erected the large dwelling-house, which stands today. Further demolition took place, and the Abbey was allowed to fall into ruins. The house and grounds were bought back by the Church in 1923, and the house is now used as a conference centre, retreat and theological training centre.

All this was on my mind as I drove through the imposing gateway and into the lovely courtyard. As I got out of the car and looked across this now dark and deserted space, I tried to picture Abbot John Paslew as he paced this area many times, deep in thought, before making his decision to light the beacon on Pendle Hill and signal the beginning of the Pilgrimage of Grace. Abbot John's ghost has been seen here in the past, and at least one person has taken a photograph of a shadowy figure, wearing a hooded robe, thought to be he.

Ian Green met me at the door, and, after he had shown me to my room, we discussed over a drink some of the peculiar happenings of the previous twelve months: doors closing by themselves, mysterious footsteps on the stone passage floors, the figure of a nun who appears periodically in the east wing.

The chef used to sleep in the room in which I was to stay and had had many experiences which were unaccountable. One night, he told me, he awoke to find a bright light shining through his window, a light with a bluish hue, which glowed brightly for some time before fading away. On other nights, he had had the feeling of someone sitting on his bed.

I learned that on one occasion a number of boy scouts, camping just outside one of the windows of these rooms, all awoke at some time during the night to find themselves surrounded by a similar fog-enshrouded light.

As Ian Green had business to attend to, I dined alone in the oak-beamed dining-room under the main hall, which looked as if it could have been the massive kitchen, when the house was first built. Certainly the floors, covered with huge flagstones, are original.

The door leading from the dining-room was a very heavy, well-mounted one, and while I sat talking with the chef after my meal, we both saw this door gradually close of its own accord. So far as I am aware, there were no draughts which could have caused this to happen, and later examination revealed that the door was hanging quite level.

The room in which I was to sleep was very cold when I retired just after midnight. Indeed, the whole of that part of the building was cold, being on ground-level and mostly of stone. Having turned in, I listened to the odd creaks and groans as the house settled down for the night, and I am sure I heard a door bang in the vicinity of the old kitchens, before I finally fell asleep.

I woke with a start at about 2.45, roused by what seemed to be a knock on my door. Investigation showed nothing but an empty passage. Then, as I started to return to my room, I heard footsteps, which approached me from the direction of the stairs near to my room. These footsteps were real to me, unhurried, steady steps which seemed to walk past me and through a locked door, fading away along the passage. I can confirm that one's hair does stand on end under these circumstances.

Apart from my hearing a door slam later, the rest of the night passed quite uneventfully.

After breakfast, I told Ian Green that I thought I had heard the footsteps. He assured me that no one had been down to my room during the night and that I had experienced something which is common to anyone who stays, or works, in that part of the house.

I like to think that these footsteps were of the past. These ghosts, whatever else they may be, are a fact of life to the staff who work at Whalley Abbey. Indeed, as I said, John Paslew's ghost has haunted this part of Whalley for years. He has been seen many times in the cloisters of the Abbot's lodgings, as well as in Wiswell Lane and Pendle Road. Were they the footsteps of John Paslew I heard in the small hours? I like to think they were.

Many of the old houses and halls of Lancashire are haunted by the ghosts of monks and priests. Small wonder, when one considers that the county was one of the great strongholds of the Catholic Faith during the period of the Reformation. Many a good priest lost his life after being betrayed for celebrating secret Masses.

The best known of these ghostly clerics are to be found six miles north of Preston, off the road from Broughton to Goosnargh, in the most famous of Lancashire's haunted sites, Chingle Hall.

It was built by Adam de Singleton in about 1258, as a small manor house of the cruciform type, surrounded by a moat, complete with drawbridge. It is thought that timbers used in the building of the house are of Norwegian oak cut from trees over a thousand years old and retrieved from vessels which had sunk in the River Ribble. Since Adam de Singleton built it, the house has seen many alterations. The cellars, recorded on the original plans, have disappeared, and the drawbridge has been replaced by a stone bridge. There is little trace of the moat; all that now remains is a small pond.

The Tudor Singletons left Chingle Hall to their younger sons, ardent Catholics, who, during the Reformation, harboured many priests in false walls built into the rooms and passages. The house is riddled with hides and escape-routes.

Chingle was next inherited by the Wall family, relatives of the Singletons, and in about 1585, despite the persecutions, it became an active Mass-centre. In a tiny signal-window in the porch, a lighted candle would indicate when Mass was about to be celebrated, and the faithful would make their way quietly over the fields and slip into the house undetected. In 1620 St John Wall was born here: he was hanged for his faith at Worcester in 1679, and it is believed that his head was brought to Chingle and buried somewhere in the cellars.

Chingle has many secrets to reveal. A medium has said that a body is buried near the window in one room, lying in the shape of a sickle. She claims that with the body are a number of valuable documents and that when these are found, the many hauntings will stop. Others believe that when the cellars are discovered and give up their secrets, things will again return to normal.

There are possibly two spectres at the hall, both monks, one believed to be Franciscan, the other dressed in a black cape and cowl. A few years ago, a wooden cross, hidden under several layers of plaster, was discovered in a small domestic chapel, and in January 1977 two cloaked and hooded figures were seen facing this cross, as if in prayer.

I am very much indebted to Mrs A. Jessop of Otumoeti, New

Zealand, for sending me much information about Michael Bingham, a young New Zealander, who flew eleven thousand miles to investigate the Chingle ghosts and spent five weeks at the Hall, recording and photographing his experiences, leaving us in no doubt that the Hall is well and truly haunted.

Nightly, Michael sat in silence waiting for the bumps and bangs and other manifestations which make the Hall famous throughout Lancashire. Some of these noises he recorded – on one occasion footsteps, which, as they came nearer to the microphone, turned into a loud buzz. Experts later confirmed that the sound could have been made only by an electro-magnetic force, which explains why cameras and tape-recorders fail to operate in certain parts of the house. Michael also photographed a face at the window, in the room over the porch, the room in which St John Wall is believed to have been born. He also filmed an apparition walking in this room. (Subsequent enquiries have revealed that the film actually broke in the camera at the point at which the figure entered the room.)

During his stay at Chingle, Michael stumbled on two more priests' hides. The first he discovered after hearing eerie footsteps in the room above the Chapel. They were heard to walk backwards and forwards across the room and then disappear into a wall. Expecting to find a body, Michael and a member of the staff began to knock away the plaster. In the process of doing this, they experienced an incredible phenomenon: they were charged by some invisible being, stamping his feet loudly on the wooden floor. They turned, expecting to see someone, but the footsteps stopped and they realized that they were the only people in the room. As they turned to continue the work in hand, the footsteps began again and only stopped when they broke through and discovered a hiding-place.

In the room where St John Wall is thought to have been born, Michael experienced other phenomena. In this room the ghost of a priest has been seen several times, and Michael experimented with its footsteps, confirming its intelligence: when he tried standing in its way, instead of walking through him, the ghost walked around him; at other times it moved to one side to avoid him!

I visited the house with a group of tourists in June 1977 and again in the early part of 1978 and confirmed Michael's experiences. One member of the household told of seeing a figure of a monk walk through the gates and into the field, but on investigation found nothing when he left the house. This same figure has been seen many times by various people, crossing the bridge and entering the porch, sometimes going up the stairs. Sounds of the dragging of some heavy object have been heard upstairs, along with rappings and tappings and footsteps which are heard quite regularly.

These and other phenomena happen at all times of the day and night, even while parties of visitors are being shown around the house. Objects move as if by invisible hands; pictures have been moved on the walls and flowers seen to be shaken in their vases. Objects are quite often and quite mysteriously thrown about the place, and people have been known to feel a friendly hand placed gently on the shoulder. One lady was actually pushed out of the way by this mysterious being, with so much force that she was propelled across the room.

Mr A. Howarth, a retired headmaster from Blackpool, told me of his experiences at Chingle, when he and a group of people visited the house in February and April 1978.

At 10 pm on the night of 3rd February one or two creaks were heard, followed by loud scratchings from one of the priests' hides in the room where Michael Bingham made his discovery. At 11.30 pm loud footsteps, slow and rather heavy, came down the lighted corridor to the door of St John Wall's bedroom. Mr Howarth was by the door when the footsetps passed him and faded into the room. No figure was seen, but the footsteps were recorded by Mr Howarth's daughter on a cassette-recorder.

The second visit they made to the Hall was on 14th April. Similar scratching and knockings were heard at about the same time, followed by the same heavy footsteps, but slightly muffled compared with the previous occasion. Again the footsteps disappeared through the door of the bedroom and were followed by knocks and scrapes, a loud bump and finally two lesser knocks, seeming as if someone had come through the wall into the priests' hide. Mr Howarth said: "In addition to this, on both occasions we have found that in one place in particular, in the priests' room, dowser rods and pendulums are activated."

There is no doubt whatsoever that Chingle Hall and an adjoining barn are haunted. Everyone I have spoken to is of the opinion that these manifestations are of St John Wall.

Not very far away, in the parish of Wesham, which stands on the

A585 a few miles north of Kirkham, one will discover what remains of the once proud home of the Westby family – Mowbreck Hall.

The Westbys were connected by marriage to the Haydocks of Cottam, ardent Catholics, two of whom died for their faith. William Haydock, a monk at Whalley Abbey, was hanged for taking part in the Pilgrimage of Grace in 1536, and George Haydock, a young priest, was betrayed, hanged, drawn and quartered in London in 1584.

George's widowed father, Vivian Haydock, who late in life also became a Jesuit priest was in hiding at Mowbreck Hall, where he performed illegal Masses in the Westbys' private chapel. On the Feast of All-Hallows Eve 1583, he stood before the small altar, robed and ready to conduct midnight Mass. Unknown to him, George was at the same time being arrested in London. As he began to say Mass, Father Vivian saw to his horror the vision of his dear son's head floating above the altar, severed, bruised and bleeding, blood trickling from his lips as they muttered the words *"Tristitia Vestra Vertetur in Gaudium"*, ("Your sadness is turning to joy"). Vivian Haydock collapsed with shock, and not long afterwards he died.

George was confined to the Tower and executed the following year. His head was preserved and today sits in a glass case in the attic chapel at Lane End House, Mawdesly. (Argument seems to surround the identity of all skulls. Some people argue that this particular one is of William Haydock.)

For well over three hundred years after the deaths of George and Vivian Haydock, people have claimed to have glimpsed manifestations of the blood-stained and dripping head, hovering open-mouthed above the Chapel altar.

In the late 1890s the Earl of Derby bought the Hall. On one occasion at that period a local dressmaker, who had to deliver an urgent order late in the evening (which meant walking the length of the tree-lined drive in the dark), arrived at the door in a state of abject terror and was only able to give the doorbell a desperate tug before collapsing in a faint on the doorstep. She could never be persuaded to reveal what had frightened her into unconsciousness, but local people nodded their heads knowingly, as they were convinced that she had seen the ghostly severed head.

During the 1960s Mowbreck Hall was converted into a country club, causing the old chapel in which Father Haydock said his last Mass to be removed. However, strange happenings caused people to wonder whether or not the place was still haunted. Unexplained footsteps, loud groans and other weird noises were very often heard. Articles vanished and re-appeared in different places, and objects were seen to move of their own accord. Unfortunately, the club closed down in 1970, and the once proud hall has since suffered much at the irresponsible hands of mindless vandals.

Another priest who left his rather unusual mark on the county was the Rev. George Marsh, the Protestant vicar of Deane.

Just a few miles north-west of Bolton stands Smithills Hall, which, if one is interested in fine architecture, is well worth a visit. Part of it is now a home for the elderly, but the remainder is open to the public.

The history of the site goes back over a thousand years. Tradition has it that a Saxon king held court here and that a chapel was consecrated about AD 790. The Knights Hospitallers of St John of Jerusalem were here in the twelfth century and are believed to have owned much of the land hereabouts.

Smithills Hall itself goes back to the fourteenth century and was built by the Radcliffe family. Over the years it has been extended, but the earlier part is of half-timbered construction. About 1516 Andrew Barton began some improvements to the house, re-building the chapel and adding a drawing-room. Andrew's son Roger made his name in a different way, by hounding the Rev. George Marsh.

Marsh, a farmer's son from a nearby village, was examined by Roger Barton and others, in the upper green chamber of the Hall, accused, as a Protestant, of being a heretic. He refused to recant or conform to the Papacy, feeling slighted and insulted, so disgusted with his treatment and the injustice of the proceedings that he swore, "Between them and me, let God witness" and, looking to Heaven, said, "If my cause be just, let the prayer of thine unworthy servant be heard." He then stamped his foot in rage on the flagstoned floor, praying that it might remain as a reminder of the injustice done to him.

After further suffering and questioning, at Lancaster Castle, George Marsh was finally burned at the stake at Chester in 1555.

The footprint is still there for all to see, a cavity in a flagstone, outside one of the doors leading to the chapel. It is said to become both wet and red once a year.

Two boys are said to have lifted the foot-printed flagstone many years ago and to have thrown it into a ditch beside the Hall. Fiendish noises were heard, terrifying everyone, until the boys confessed and the stone was replaced.

On a number of occasions a figure has been seen which is thought to be the ghost of Marsh himself: the apparition of a man dressed in white vestments of the period, holding a book in his hand, glides between the corridors and court-room of the Hall.

Nathaniel Hawthorne, when US Consul at Liverpool, visited the Hall in 1856 and wrote luridly about the footprint, but he gave a Hollywood-type version of how the footprint came into being.

According to him, an old Lord of Smithills became obsessed with the idea that he could live forever, provided a human life was sacrificed for him once every thirty years. The old Lord was the guardian of a young and beautiful orphan girl, and one day she was lured by him into the nearby woods, where he slew her, burying her corpse on the spot. Every step taken by the Lord from then on left behind a bloody footprint, which followed him through the woods, up the stairs of the Hall and into his bedroom. Horrified, the old Lord fled from the Hall, but the bloody trail followed him, even as far as the King's Court. Now half crazed, he never returned to Smithills Hall and, according to Hawthorne, was never heard of again, but the footprint has remained ever since, as a reminder of man's folly.

The Lune banks are thick with Anglian names: Clapham, High Bentham, Tatham and Melling. It was here, in this quiet village of gracious old houses and cottages, that I met John and Mary Mulroy at their charming old cottage opposite the Norman church, and heard of their remarkable ghost, that of a friendly old canon.

Todd Cottage, the Mulroys' lovely home, was built, according to the builder's mark over the door, in 1687. (The deeds go back to 1700.) The word *tod* in Old English means 'fox', and presumably this was originally 'Fox Cottage', the extra letter being added with time. For many years the cottage was owned by Mrs Mulroy's parents, and before them the tenants were the Bells and the Culpins.

So far as is known, there are no records of previous tenants having seen or heard ghosts, and Mr Mulroy seems to be the one who has brought on these manifestations, for a reason which we will examine later. He says he has always been sceptical about ghosts and hauntings, but the events over the past few years have convinced him that such things are possible.

One night he was surprised to see a figure suddenly appear and stand alongside his bed — surprised, to say the least. By the way the figure was dressed, in the old-style clerical dress and dog-collar, he thought for a moment that it was his old Chinese steward standing alongside him. He told me: "I was wide awake. In fact, I hadn't been asleep. The figure was rather fuzzy, and I could not make out the face. After looking at me for a minute or two, he vanished."

The figure appeared quite regularly after that, and in time Mr Mulroy was able to see his face quite clearly. Not having seen or heard any reference to a ghost in the cottage, he happened one day to mention his experiences to the vicar and was able to describe the figure. The vicar suggested he should go across to the church and take a look at an old photograph on the wall of the vestry. There, in an old gilt frame, he was surprised to see the face of his apparition looking down at him from the vestry wall. The photograph was of a canon who had lived in the village at the turn of the century.

For the first two years, from January to March, the ghost appeared quite frequently, and although his wife did not see it, or feel its presence, Mr Mulroy became quite used to him. Except for two occasions when he held up his arms as if in blessing, the figure never moved, and he was always silent. Recently he has started appearing more frequently than before and during the daylight hours.

"Last winter, at about seven o'clock one evening, I had occasion to go up to the bedroom," Mr Mulroy said. "It was quite dark, and, as I entered the room, I saw a figure behind the door. Thinking it might be an intruder, I struck out at him with my fist. He appeared so solid, I was sure it was a human being." However, his fist went straight through the figure, striking the wall, and only then did he realize what it was. Mr Mulroy laughed: "I even apologized to him when I saw who it was."

Mr Mulroy is sure the ghost knows of his own presence. By his expression the ghost always appears benevolent, and as there does not seem to be anything nasty or vicious about him, he has come to be regarded with the same affection as the family cat.

When the apparition appears, there does not seem to be any change in the temperature, nor any air disturbance, and because of this, it was at first thought it might be marsh gases making their way upstairs and giving off a phosphorescent glow. But then the figure appeared and was far too solid-looking. The fact that it appears in the daylight spoils this theory anyway.

Mr Mulroy was kind enough to take me over to the vestry to look at the photograph of the Canon. He was the Rev. B. Grenside, vicar of Melling from 1855 until his death in 1913, made honorary Canon of Manchester in 1905. From his photograph he appears to be a typical Victorian preacher of the 'hellfire and brimstone' variety. His eyes, however, give away the fact that he was probably a very kind and sympathetic person. He was well respected in the village during his lifetime and is still remembered with affection by a few of the older residents. That he was a tough old boy is obvious. He was very keen on hunting, shooting, fishing and riding, and it was as a result of a fall while riding that he died and was buried in the churchyard overlooking the cottage.

There are two theories held locally as to why the friendly ghost haunts Todd Cottage. One is that the old Canon wanted to buy the cottage but for some reason or another was never able to persuade the owners to sell. The other, held by Mr Mulroy, is to do with himself.

Mr Mulroy is a Roman Catholic, whereas his wife, Mary, is Church of England and the daughter of a vicar. During the Canon's day, a marriage of this nature would have been out of the question as there was a very wide gap between the two religions, particularly in a village as small and close as this one – hence the ghost's appearance, to inspect the ecumenical phenomenon.

I spent a most enjoyable day at Todd Cottage, but at the time of my visit the Canon did not oblige us with a visit. However, Mr Mulroy wrote to me a few days later to tell me that no sooner had my car got out of sight than the old Canon appeared at his side. Perhaps he too was seeing me off.

Our final ghost in this section haunts a school in North Road, St Helens, once a convent attached to Lowe House Roman Catholic Church. Recent pupils are familiar with a ghost which has appeared quite frequently in, of all places, an upstairs toilet, which is apparently on the site of an earlier dormitory. No one knows the origin of this ghost, but unlike the others in this chapter, she appears dressed in the habit of a nun.

10

THE MAN IN THE STREET

Haunted houses, castles and country homes are not the only places where one is likely to come across ghostly apparitions. One can meet them in the most unlikely places, for instance in a public park, down a country lane and even in the city street.

At about 10.30 pm on a night in the winter of 1976, Josephine Whitehead was walking through Lancaster, her thoughts on the events of the evening. It was a cold night, the wind blowing cold and damp. She would not be sorry to reach the comparative warmth of the car, which was parked near Lancaster Castle. She made her way towards the Judge's Lodgings at the top of Church Street, a steep road leading up to the castle and one of the oldest parts of the city. Houses and shops had stood in this road from medieval times, and there had probably been houses here before then. Now, many of them were boarded up and derelict, awaiting the hammer of the demolition men.

As she walked along the road, Mrs Whitehead noticed a man walking about ten yards or so ahead of her. She had not noticed him before, and she followed him without taking much interest. Halfway up, he stopped and entered one of the houses, which surprised her, because she knew they were supposed to be boarded up.

Her curiosity now aroused, Mrs Whitehead made towards the house, wondering if perhaps it had been renovated and now had new tenants. To her amazement, the door through which the man had entered was boarded up. "No one," she says, "Could have gotten into that house. I tried myself, but it was not possible." She was left with the realization that whoever she had followed had passed right through the boarded-up door. There was no other entrance. He could not have entered the house on either side, because they were boarded up in the same way.

Not many miles away, at Yealand Conyers, they tell the story of a similar phenomenon, which has still not been explained. A woman, returning home late one night from Warton, was passing Warton Woods when a spectre, which she was unable to define, took her by the arm and escorted her along the lonely road, to within sight of the first house in Yealand Conyers. Many years ago, another ghost was reported, which walked Peter Lane, the old coach-road through Yealand Conyers.

Green Lane, at Galgate, south of Lancaster, was the scene of a terrible murder well over a century ago, which consequently gave rise to the name 'Murder Lane'. A servant-girl walking along this lane was attacked and murdered. The following morning, her body was found, covered by a thin layer of snow. Every year, on the anniversary of her death, there is said to be a layer of snow at this spot in Green Lane. A worn memorial now marks the spot where the body was found.

A few miles down the road at Garstang, there is a bridge which is said to be guarded by the ghost of a woman murdered here many years ago, which takes the form of a skeleton in a cloak and hood. She used to hitch lifts from horsemen as they crossed the bridge and only revealed her true identity when she was safely mounted behind the rider and the horse was on its way. Then, with a hideous cackle, she would whip the horse into a frenzied gallop and cling with cold, clammy hands to the rider's back. The rider would inevitably faint with terror and would be thrown from the horse and injured or killed.

At Penwortham Wood one might come across the Fairy Funeral, which, it is said, will forecast the death of whoever is witness to it. Two men were unlucky enough to meet the tiny cortège as they returned home one night. The funeral procession was seen to emerge from the churchyard. One of the men, to his horror, was able to see the figure in the tiny coffin and recognized the face of the corpse as his own. Within a few weeks he fell from a haystack onto a pitchfork, which pierced his stomach and killed him. His funeral passed along the very same route as the fairy funeral procession.

Delph Lane in Whiston harbours the ghost of a young seaman, who some years ago, after doing a spot of courting, left his girl at her doorway and made his way home through the old stone-quarry. Unfortunately he missed his footing in the dark and plunged over a hundred feet to his death at the bottom of the quarry. Around 1945, a

⁄ returning home one night when, as she passed the
⁄eading to the quarry, she saw a man on the footpath. She
⁄in a few yards of him when he mysteriously vanished. So far
⁄n aware, this ghost has never been seen since.

Castle Hill, on the boundary between Golbourne and Newton-le-
Willows, has been haunted for many years by a spectre known locally
as 'the White Lady'. This ghost has been seen many times over the
past thirty years or so, either as a white shape in the woods or as a
motionless figure, nearly six feet tall, wearing what appears to be a
monk's habit and standing with arms folded.

A few years ago 'she' drifted out in front of a motor-cyclist on his
way home from Golbourne, late one night. A white arm wrapped itself
around his neck and hurled him from his machine. Covered in cuts
and bruises, he wasted no time in running home, returning the
following day with the police to retrieve his damaged machine.

'The White Lady' is also reported to have appeared to pedestrians
and has materialized suddenly in the headlights of cars, causing them
to swerve or even crash. Sometime during the 1960s a young man
reported seeing the ghost as he cycled home near this spot late one
night. In the beam of his bicycle lamp he picked up what appeared to
be a huge figure, dressed in white and larger than the average man.
The figure remained motionless for some time, whereas the poor
cyclist pedalled like fury until he reached the comparative safety of the
East Lancashire Road, a few hundred yards away.

I am informed that, since the M6 was built, the ghost has not been
seen as frequently, although 'she' has been spotted at least once,
floating across the motorway. Who was she? So far as local legend
goes, 'she' was the victim of some local romantic tragedy, who now
grieves for her lost lover's soul.

During the latter part of the nineteenth century, the people of the
Everton district of Liverpool became quite used to seeing the energetic
ghost which became known as 'Spring-Heeled Jack' who was said to
jump, in thirty-foot leaps, around William Henry Street.

Bibby's Lane in Bootle is a place to avoid, unless you wish to come
across the ghost of John Bibby, who has been reported many times
driving along the lane in his four-in-hand, with his head tucked
underneath his arm.

The blitz of May 1941 will long live in the memory and last in the history of Liverpool. It was the worst week of sustained raids on any part of Britain, an all-out attempt by the German Luftwaffe to wreck the port from which Western Approaches Command controlled the convoy system which fed the nation.

During one of these raids several hundred people were killed in the Lawrence Gardens area of the city, amongst them a well-loved and much-respected policeman who, oblivious of his own safety, was blown to pieces while patrolling the area in the pitch-black night, tapping his truncheon on walls and railings to guide his way.

About ten years ago, several residents in the area reported seeing a figure dressed in the old-fashioned police uniform, wearing a tin hat and carrying what looked like an old gas-mask case, making his way along the dark streets, tapping his truncheon on walls and railings as he went along. Some hardy souls are reported to have tried to catch up with him, but as they approached, he always disappeared into thin air.

Five miles north-west of Clitheroe stands the pretty little village of Bashall Eaves, traditionally associated with King Arthur, who is thought to have fought a battle here. Beyond Bashall Eaves lies the Forest of Bowland. This is Lancashire witch-country, a place of fiercely independent people who dislike change and resent outside interference. Many a poor wretch has been brought through this area to be tried and executed at Lancaster, after being accused of witchcraft. It is not surprising, therefore, that some ghost-stories may have been put about to keep away strangers.

A murder was committed here in 1934 which remains not only unsolved but as baffling today as it was forty years ago.

One Sunday evening, John Dawson, a middle-aged bachelor farmer, followed his usual custom of visiting his local pub, returning to the farm at about ten o'clock. As he passed through the gate, he felt a sharp blow on the back, but looking around, he saw no one and, thinking that someone had thrown a stone at him, he ignored the incident. He then had supper with his sister and retired to bed. During the night, John's shoulder became painful, and as the pain became unbearable, he realized that he might possibly be injured, but even then he decided to do nothing about it until morning.

The following morning, the pain was intense, and he asked his sister to look at his back. There was good reason. A ragged wound spread downwards from his left shoulder-blade. His horrified sister called the doctor, who immediately had him removed to Blackburn Royal Infirmary and notified the local police. Three days later, John Dawson died.

At the inquest, it was revealed that he had been killed by a large bullet which had lodged near his liver. It appeared that the bullet had been specially made and cut from a piece of steel on a lathe.

Every person in the area who was in possession of a shot-gun was called in by the police for examination. Every workshop, garden-hut and tool-shed which might have held a lathe was searched, but not one single clue was uncovered.

Today there are many stories told of a squat figure, with a gaping wound showing through his tattered coat as he passes through the hedge near the farm, sometimes bending over, seeking in vain for the weapon and the person who used it. Is it any wonder that local people are not too keen on passing along the road taken by John Dawson on that fateful night in the spring of 1934?

There are, of course, numerous ghosts in this part of the county. Perhaps one of the best-known ghosts in Clitheroe was that of a man who was murdered years ago on the bridge. Since his murder, bloodstains have appeared for a good number of years on the spot where he died, usually on the anniversary of his death. The corpse was moved about quite often just after murder, but finally, I believe, it was left in the old bonehouse, where it was eventually discovered by some boys from the Clitheroe Grammar School, which stood in the churchyard. I am told that nothing would grow in the hedge through which the body had been dragged before being thrown into the ditch, and his ghost was frequently seen in the vicinity of the bridge.

Ghosts from the Civil War are common in Lancashire: in 1648, Cromwell routed the Royalists along the Lancashire plain, from Maghull in the north to Warrington in the south-east. The many alleged hauntings by Cavaliers testify to this black period of our history, but for some strange reason I am unable to find any evidence to suggest that Parliamentarians' ghosts haunt the area.

At Maghull, north of Liverpool, the sound of galloping horses and the clash of accoutrements can be heard just to the south of the town, a phenomenon heard many times usually at dusk. Sometimes, against a grey stone wall, the spectres of headless horsemen can be seen. They may be the remnants of the Royalist army fleeing south, or, it has been suggested, the ghosts of Jacobites who tried to escape when Preston was recaptured in 1715.

A few miles away, at Newton-le-Willows, the ghosts of Royalists caught and hanged by Cromwell are still to be heard marching to their doom, while on the edge of Turton Moors, above Bolton, a Cavalier has been seen to materialize out of the wall of some old cottages, and in broad daylight. Near this spot the sound of marching feet has been heard going past the cottages, and voices of invisible beings speaking of 'menace' and 'peril'.

St Mary's churchyard at Rochdale has a sinister apparition which is seen quite often – the last time about four years ago. A man dressed in knee-breeches has been seen gliding from the graveyard to the nearby river. Several people, including local policemen, have seen the ghost, a strange and silent figure which appears to float above the surface of the ground. In 1974 the graveyard was cleared for a new road to go through, and now the area has been completely rebuilt, but the apparition is still seen drifting across the area after dark.

Bleak Rivington village, near Horwich, has a ghostly horseman who is said to ride an old lane within the precincts of the vicarage garden. Only his head can be seen, the ghostly body and horse hidden by the now sunken lane. Another apparition to be encountered at Rivington is said to be of a priest who forgot where he had hidden the church treasures from Thomas Cromwell. Rivington Moor, a desolate place, is haunted by a spectral horseman, dressed in black, whose evil-looking nag could tread through the bog without even getting its feet wet.

The place known as 'Scotsman's Stump', which is near Rivington Pike, is haunted by the victim of an unsolved murder, committed here in the early part of the nineteenth century. The victim's ghost is said to visit the scene from time to time.

Turton Tower has a rather spectacular ghost, or rather ghosts, for these take the form of a phantom coach and horses, which people claim to have seen driving across the moors on an old Roman road, through what is now a private house but was once a barn. It carries on until it reaches the old entrance to Turton Tower, where it suddenly vanishes.

Belmont Road, Bolton, was once the haunt of a highwayman by the name of Horrocks. Once, after holding up a coach, he was surprised by the sudden arrival of a young traveller named Grimshaw. In his haste to get away, Horrocks threw the booty into the bushes and marked the spot, intending to return for it when the coast was clear. However, the young Grimshaw saw a piece of jewellery glistening in the moonlight and, on investigation, discovered the proceeds of the robbery. Instead of handing the property over to the authorities as soon as possible, the young man kept it, in the hope of turning it into easy money. But he made the mistake of trying to sell some of the jewellery from the haul in a local tavern, where he was seen by a thief-taker and was arrested. He was dragged before the magistrate and charged with highway robbery. At his trial, his story about finding the stolen goods was disbelieved, and he was found guilty and hanged at Preston in 1780.

It is the ghost of the unfortunate Grimshaw that is said to haunt the Belmont Road area, with a piece of gallows-rope around his neck, his eyes popping out 'like organ stops', trying to protest his innocence, although no words come out of the gaping mouth, and no sound is heard as he roams the area on dark nights.

Still in Bolton, Deane Road is said to be haunted by an unidentified ghost allegedly associated with the Institute of Technology. Apparently, to build the Institute, it was necessary to knock down a number of small workshops which had stood on that site for many years, and locals think the ghost is of someone who was a worker there.

He was seen in the summer of 1970, wearing a white shirt and dark grey trousers, standing on the College lawn. At first the figure was thought to be the caretaker, he looked so normal – tall, thin and possibly middle-aged, with thinning dark hair. On being approached, he suddenly disappeared.

Several local residents have seen this ghost, the last time being one evening during the summer of 1977.

Next, a haunting in Manchester, which serves as a reminder of a foul deed perpetrated 150 years ago.

William Wood, a clothing manufacturer, was returning home after doing business in Manchester one autumn night in 1823 when, just outside Disley, he was accosted by three footpads. After refusing their demands for money, Mr Wood was set upon and viciously assaulted. Throwing their victim to the ground, they battered him insensible, finally crushing his skull with a heavy rock.

The ground was reasonably hard, but so severe was the battering to his head that it left an impression, a cavity, four inches deep by about sixteen to eighteen inches in diameter.

Early the following morning a passing carrier discovered the corpse, which he picked up and carried to 'The Jodrell Arms' at Whaley Bridge, demanding of a servant that he inform the authorities at once. Very soon a full-scale investigation was under way, and it was not long before one of the attackers, Robert Dale, was arrested and charged with the offence. The other two were never found. Dale would reveal neither their names nor their whereabouts, and subsequently he was tried, convicted and hanged at Chester on 21st April 1824.

Meanwhile, the mortal remains of the unfortunate Mr Wood were buried, and in 1874 a stone was erected on the spot where he was murdered.

The story goes that the hole in the ground which was made by his head during the savage attack remained barren after his death. Nothing, not even a blade of grass, would grow there, and it was also found to be impossible to fill the hole with stones or soil. Someone tried to fill it in several years later with gravel and stones, but they were found shortly afterwards scattered in all directions. After this, many attempts were made to fill it in or cover it with turf, but in spite of all these efforts, it proved to be a fruitless task. Once the hole was tightly packed with stones, rammed tightly home, and the whole area covered with turf: the following day, the hole was again empty, as though William Wood wished it to remain a silent reminder of the foul deed committed there, that fateful night in 1823.

Forever afterwards, the spot was said to be haunted, and most local people, knowing of its association with the murder, consider it wise to avoid the area after darkness has fallen. Coincidentally, the case was brought to light again in 1855, when a man is said to have made a death-bed confession admitting his complicity in the murder of Mr Wood.

Until it was demolished and a modern block of flats built on the site, a charming seventeenth-century thatched cottage, Fancy Lodge, stood in Hey Houses, near Lytham. The cottage was well-known as a haunted site, and passers-by became quite used to seeing the apparition of the lady in white, who, if spoken to or approached, would suddenly disappear.

In an earlier chapter I mentioned the ghost of a Victorian child at Colne Hall. A couple of miles away, at Laneshaw Bridge, there is another, older ghost, the victim of a murder committed one Sunday in July 1789. The girl, Hannah Corbridge, left her home on the fateful Sunday evening with her boyfriend, Christopher Hartley, by whom she was alleged to be pregnant. Hannah did not return home that night, nor for the next two or three, when her distraught father set out with some local men to search the countryside for her.

Not far from her home she was found dead in a ditch. She had been poisoned, and her throat had been cut with enough ferocity to all but decapitate her. Hartley was immediately suspected, and when arrested he soon confessed to having murdered the poor girl. He appears to have tried to poison her but, the poison having too slow a reaction, he panicked and cut Hannah's throat, throwing the body into an old trunk at his home before burying it in the ditch near Barnside Hall. Tradition has it that a local villager had a dream in which he saw where the body had been buried, and so was able to tell Hannah's father exactly where to look.

Hannah's ghost was often seen, for a number of years after, usually on Sunday evenings, around the spot where the murder took place. She is said to have appeared so regularly that the tenants of Barnside Hall sent for the local parish priest to exorcize her. He seems to have had little success, for I heard only recently from a man who swears he has seen Hannah's ghost as recently as 1964, close to Laneshaw Bridge itself, which is very interesting, because years after the murder Barnside Hall was pulled down and some of the stones were used to repair Laneshaw Bridge. I am told that sometimes there was a reddish appearance to several of the stones, and people said that, after the murder, Hartley wiped the blood of Hannah from his hands by rubbing them on the stones of the Hall and that it had seeped into the stonework only to be washed out by the waters of the stream that rushes under Laneshaw Bridge.

PART TWO
Traditional Ghosts, Boggarts and Legends

The storm will arise, and trouble the skies;
This night, and more for the wonder,
The ghost from the tomb, affronted shall come,
Called out by the clap of the thunder.

                              Robert Herrick

TRADITIONAL GHOSTS, BOGGARTS AND LEGENDS

Every county has its popular ghosts and legends, stories which have been passed down from generation to generation. Legends and traditions are rapidly disappearing in this enlightened age, but fortunately many of the ghosts remain. Some of them pass away with the ancient homes to which they were associated, it is true, but others have survived and brought a hint of respectability to their haunts. So, in writing about the ghosts and legends of Lancashire, one must not overlook the traditional ones, the ghosts and legends of before the Industrial Revolution.

Even though Lancashire is a hive of industry and commerce, no one can stroll very far from our towns without discovering some of the earthy qualities and virtues that stem from a deep and near-religious respect for the soil.

When the industrialists, the capitalist revolutionaries of the seventeenth century, built for themselves a harsh commercial world and put woman and children down the coal-mines and into the dark satanic mills, they were aware of three qualities firmly rooted in the people: staunchness, firmness and a great sense of pride. Is it any wonder then that tales and legends sprang as much from the cities and industrial towns of Lancashire, as from the farmlands along the Fylde and the slopes of Pendle? Farmers, weavers, miners – they all had heroes of their own to sing and talk about and with whom they could identify.

This being a county long associated with witchcraft, no book of this nature would be complete without some mention of the legends and superstitions surrounding the countryside around Pendle, and of the Hell Hounds and boggarts who have had tales told about them for centuries.

In the following chapters, I have tried to bring together as many of these legends as time and resources permit. As they are a part of our Lancashire heritage, I hope the reader will not feel cheated if I give them a further airing. If I have left out the reader's favourite ghost or legend, I apologize, but to write of all the ghosts and legends in the county would, in itself, be a lifetime's work. Here I have written about the ghosts of the big houses and areas of Lancashire that I have visited personally and which to my mind represent some of the darker aspects of our history.

11

BOGGARTS

I think it was Walter Greenwood who described the boggart as "a mischievous night-marauding gnome". It has also been described as 'an evil spirit'. The word 'boggart' is really a corruption of the Old English *bar gaist*, which is itself a modification of *burgh gaist* – *burgh* meaning 'town', and *gaist* being an old North Country expression for 'ghost'. Hence *burgh gaist*, 'town ghost', soon became corrupted to 'boggart'.

There are boggarts aplenty, from one end of the county to the other, such as the boggart at Stalmine, near Poulton-le-Fylde, known as 'the Hall Knocker'. This helpful spirit gathered in the marsh sheep, mucked out shippens and in general made himself useful around the local farms. He is reputed to lie beneath the threshold stone of the local church.

At Clayton Hall, Droylsden, a night-time boggart disturbed the residents by rattling chains, dragging heavy weights about and making sleep impossible by pulling off the bedclothes. In the end, a young clergyman is said to have exorcized it by pronouncing, "Whilst ivy climbs and holly is green, Clayton Hall boggart shall no more be seen." It is said to have worked, as no one has seen or heard the spirit at least within living memory.

In the first half of the nineteenth century, a man living at Burnley Wood was driven from his home by a boggart, who refused to let him sleep at night, until finally he had to move out of the house.

Boggart Hole Clough, on the outskirts of Manchester, was the den of one well-known boggart. Many years ago, in a nearby dell stood a farm which belonged to a farmer by the name of George Cheetham. He and his family were tormented by a boggart who took up permanent residence at the farm. Whenever the family were sitting around the big kitchen fire telling amusing stories, the cheeky imp's shrill laughter could be heard mingling with that of the family.

One evening, after the laughter had been heard again, Robert, the youngest and most adventurous of the farmer's sons, demanded in a loud voice that the boggart stop hiding in a cowardly manner and show himself. The laughter abruptly stopped, but when Robert and his brothers were asleep later that night, they were dragged from their beds by unseen hands and heard the boggart laughing gleefully at their discomfort. The next night, the farmer insisted that the boys sleep in the carthouse for safety, and they duly moved out of their room. This pleased the boggart. Now he had his own room and could consider himself a member of the family and not just a visitor. As such, he did on occasion help around the house, churning the cream and cleaning the pans, but he remained as mischievous as ever, clattering up and down stairs, throwing pots and pans about, pulling the children's bedclothes off at night and, on one occasion, throwing a shoe-horn at the head of one of the children.

Finally George decided that enough was enough and that if the uninvited guest would not move way, then the family would. Moving-day arrived and George and his sons loaded the cart with the family possessions. Just as they were putting the last piece on the cart, a neighbour called, and George explained to him that they were moving to get away from the tiresome spirit. As he finished speaking, a little voice called out, "Aye neighbour, we're flitting!" Resignedly, George and his wife looked at each other, and, realizing the futility of moving, they wearily unpacked all their furniture and put it back into the house. After that day the boggart never bothered the family again.

Unfortunately the farm no longer remains, and most of the land is now part of one of the Manchester parks, where today people enjoy fishing, boating and other leisure activities. but they do say that if anyone tells an amusing tale in the dell, shrill laughter may still be heard from time to time.

Well Hall, near Clitheroe, had a boggart of a sociable disposition, who used to keep an old woman company by the fireside on long winter nights. Although friendly towards the old woman, he is claimed to have once chained a man to the wall in his temper.

Towneley Hall, Burnley, had a cheeky boggart who usually hung about around the bridge, scaring the daylights out of the unfortunate locals who were forced to use it. Eventually the Towneley priest was persuaded to go out to the nearby clough where the boggart lived to exorcize him. Sallying forth, fortified by the Church and no doubt by something stronger than Communion wine, the priest set out to 'lay' the tiresome boggart. He was not entirely successful, for the boggart made certain conditions to which the priest agreed: the boggart promised never to appear again providing that on one day each year he might have the life of the first person to cross the bridge, for as long as a green leaf grew in the clough.

In order to ensure peace, every year it was the custom to sacrifice a chicken on the boggart's day, and to ensure a supply of year-round leaves, the clough was planted with holly trees, or hollins. To this day, the area is known as 'Hollinhey Clough'.

At Longridge, just off Dilworth Road, there is a heavy stone slab which is said to have been the prison of a boggart for over three hundred years. There is an inscription on the stone which reads;

RAVFFE: RADCLIFFE: LAID: THIS: STONE:
TO: LYE: FOR: EVER: A: D: 1655.

Tradition has it that the area was haunted by a nasty, spiteful boggart that not only molested travellers by scratching, pinching and punching them but was also responsible for screeching noises which frightened any passing horse and caused several people to die of fright.

Nearby stands a farmhouse which was owned by a family called Radcliffe who seemed to have been particularly plagued by a boggart, which, it is said, Ralph Radcliffe imprisoned under this stone after several of his family died quite suddenly.

A later owner of the farm, seeing the slab, decided he could make better use of it at the farm and sent several of his men and a team of horses to collect it from the lane. The men and horses struggled and pulled for most of the day, until it was finally freed and taken to the farm, where it was set in the dairy. Then the farmer had nothing but trouble. Nothing could be placed on it without falling over; it never settled; people were forever catching shins or ankles on it, and anyone who sat on it was more than likely to become ill within a few hours. So the farmer decided to put the stone back where he had found it, hoping to appease the boggart, and although he expected a hard task ahead of him when it came to moving it back, he was surprised when the return journey was accomplished with remarkable ease. In fact, it was returned in less than a quarter of the time it took to bring it, and only one horse was needed.

A local doctor poured scorn on the legend of the written stone and is said to have ridden out to issue a challenge, but when he came within sight of the stone, a shapeless form arose out of it, dragging him from his frightened horse, trying to choke the life out of him. Fortunately, the doctor managed to free himself and take hold of his terrified horse. He threw himself into the saddle and was two or three miles further down the road before he could manage to stop the horse. After that the doctor rarely spoke of his experience, but he never scoffed about the stone again.

Although it has been established that the legend of the Clegg Hall boggart was used as a cover-up for illicit coining during the Commonwealth period, it seems certain that a ghost did exist at some time on the site of the old Hall.

Clegg Hall, at Milnrow, near Rochdale, is now, alas, a ruin, but its boggart is famous throughout Lancashire. He is said to have come about as the result of a brutal murder, committed in the fourteenth century, on the site of an earlier house. It is the traditional tale of a wicked uncle who murdered the two young heirs to the House, after they had been orphaned and put in his care. He is said to have thrown them over a balcony and into a moat, where they subsequently drowned. Even though the original house was pulled down, the site was still said to be haunted by the evil spirit.

Some years after the new house had been built on this site, round about the year 1620, Nicholas and Alice Haworth, brother and sister, owners of Clegg Hall, were setting out to a marriage-ball at Stubley, near Todmorden, when, driving through their gardens, they met a ragged beggar, who by some means or other managed to gain not only food but lodging at the Hall.

During the ball, later in the evening, two strangers arrived and, to the delight of the assembled guests, performed conjuring tricks. One of the conjurors singled Alice out from the other dancers, and a mechanical bird gave her a message in its beak, telling her to go to the haunted room at Clegg Hall at midnight the following night – and to go alone. This was the room where the boggart was said to live and where Nicholas had lodged the beggar.

The following night, her curiosity aroused, Alice went to the haunted room, a few minutes after midnight. As she entered, the candle she was carrying was blown out, and she was seized in the darkness and carried protesting through the various passages to the cellar. When her mysterious assailants had left her, and her eyes became accustomed to the gloom, she found, to her surprise, that she was surrounded by hoards of foreign coins. The conjuror who had given her the message at the ball suddenly appeared and to her further surprise told her that he was madly in love with her and that, if she would marry him, she could have all the money which surrounded her.

The following morning Alice was nowhere to be found. The beggar told Nicholas that he feared she was being held by the boggart and offered to try, for a price, to exorcize the spirits, which, he said, were of the two children murdered over three hundred years before. If these spirits were appeased, Alice would return safely.

Later in the day, the beggar, having obtained permission from Nicholas, ordered the sacrificing of a cockerel, which he later quartered and buried. Soon there was a loud explosion, and the beggar ran to the haunted room, returning with Alice in his arms.

It was later discovered that the beggar and his son and an accomplice had been making counterfeit money in the cellars of the house. The beggar, who turned out to be called Clegg, had hoped to drive Alice and Nicholas out of the house with the tales of boggarts and ghosts and thereby gain possession of Clegg Hall, his ancestral home. His plan would probably have succeeded but for his son falling in love with Alice. As it was, the house was pulled down and destroyed, and the large hoard of counterfeit money was destroyed with it.

Of course, anyone will tell you that boggarts can take many forms and, like the witch's familiar, the humble cat has often been suspected of not being what he seems. Take this traditional story which goes back many years and has been told by scores of Lancashire grandmothers to their wide-eyed grandchildren – a fact borne out recently when I heard it re-told to a group of Space Age children in Burnley. Judging by their expressions, they were as impressed as their grandparents and great-grandparents had been, when they first heard it.

One evening, an old Lancashire farmer dropped wearily into his chair beside the big open farm-kitchen fire, in front of which slept his big black cat. The farmer, shaking his head and scratching his chin, said to his wife, "I dunno lass, I've just seen t'funniest thing I've ever seen in me life!" He went on to tell her how, on his way home, he was walking past a hedge when he stopped to fasten his leggings. At the other side of the hedge he heard the sound of marching feet – not the sound of men marching but of small animals on the dead leaves in the hedge bottom. He got up slowly and peered through the hedge. There he saw twelve black cats walking on their hind-legs and carrying a small coffin. Leading them was a big white cat, which miaowed with every ten steps he took. The farmer was dumbfounded. When the procession came abreast of him, the white cat spotted him and, turning to the others, lifted his paw. The twelve black cats stopped, putting the coffin down. Then all thirteen cats stood looking at the farmer.

As he told his story, the farmer's cat began to stir on the hearth, and as he continued, his cat seemed to be growing bigger and bigger.

The farmer went on to say that the white cat spoke to him and said, "You! Go and tell Dildrum, Doldrum's dead!" At this, the farmer's cat sat bolt upright and said, "What? Doldrum dead? Then I'm the king of the cats!" As soon as he had spoken, the cat disappeared with a great 'whoosh' up the chimney, and neither the farmer nor his wife saw or heard of him again!

There were several other places, especially in East Lancashire, where boggarts might be met. At Worsthorne, Burnley, one old man known as 'Johnnie o' th' Pasture' is said to have met a black dog to whom he bartered his soul. At the bottom of Brunshaw in the vicinity of Turf Moor, the hallowed ground of Burnley Football Club, one might meet the 'Bee Hole' boggart which is reported to have carried off an old woman, only leaving her skin on a thornbush to show what had happened.

Barcroft Hall, at Walk Mill near Todmorden, had a boggart known as 'Hob o' th' Hurst', who was said to have been nice and friendly at first and to have assisted the Barcroft family in every possible way. Unfortunately, one of the Barcrofts presented the visitor with a pair of clogs to show the family's appreciation of his help, and from then on the boggart changed and began to play the most mischievous tricks. Perhaps the anonymous donor should have remembered that no boggart or witch could harm anyone until he or she had received a present from that person!

It is said that some poachers caught a boggart in their net at Barley and that boggarts and fairies have been seen at Hey Well near Cockden and at Jam Hole Well at Worsthorne, where they made little pats of butter. In 1829 a woman claimed to have seen some fairies playing in a field at Brownside.

12

THE DEVIL VISITS LANCASHIRE

Legends concerning the Devil are many in this part of the world. The keep at Clitheroe Castle has a window said to have been made by the Devil tossing rocks from Pendle Hill. He is also said to have stalked the streets of Clitheroe waylaying the townsfolk and offering three wishes for their soul; eventually he was defeated by the townsfolk and is said to have vanished, in a fit of pique, at Hell Hole Bridge.

He popped up again during the last century in the Rossendale Valley, where the favourite pastime has always been football and where, much to the dismay of local clergy, lads committed the ultimate sin of playing on Sundays – that is, until one Sunday when the Devil joined in a game at Crawshawbooth: he gave the ball a mighty kick, sending it way up into the sky; there was a flash of fire, and the smell of brimstone and sulphur, and the terrified locals vowed they would never again play football on a Sunday.

The old Burnley Grammar School, which stands next to the parish church, is said to have been the scene of a visit from the Prince of Darkness himself.

Some of the boys discovered an old book containing spells and charms, among which they found a reference to means of raising the Devil. Like most schoolboys, they were curious as to the effects this spell would have and decided to try it out.

One day, when there were no masters present, the boys gathered in one of the old classrooms, and the most daring of them began to weave a spell, following the directions laid down in the book. He carved circles in the air with his arm, making strange passes with his hands and muttering many incantations. At last he came to the most important part of the charm. Taking up the Lord's Prayer, he began to recite it backwards as fast as he could. When he reached the end of the

Old Burnley Grammar School, where schoolboys are said to have raised the Devil. A black mark can still be seen on the flagstones where he is said to have risen.

Haigh Hall, Wigan. It was from this site that Lady Dorothy set out to do her weekly penance, in rags and barefooted, to Mab's Cross, two miles away.

Samlesbury Hall. The ghost of the White Lady of Samlesbury has often been seen drifting across this courtyard after dark.

charm, to the astonishment and horror of all the boys present, before their eyes one of the flagstones moved, tilted and lifted up, and out popped the black, horned head of the Devil himself. Half the boys fled in terror, but one bold spirit seized a hammer that lay nearby and gave the Devil such a bang on the head that he yelled out in pain and drew back. Seeing him flinch, the other boys set about him in earnest. With hammer and tongs, clogs, fists and anything they could lay hands on, the boys beat him as hard as they could. Such a walloping from a score of Lancashire clogs and fists was more than even the Devil could stand. He gave a howl and vanished. The Devil was never seen in Burnley again after that day.

Sceptical? Next time you are in the vicinity, call into the old school, which is now used as offices by the Education Department, and ask them to explain the black mark clearly visible on the flagstones. They will tell you that the mark was made by the Prince of Darkness himself as he rose through the floor, at this very spot.

The idea of outwitting the Devil caused amusement around countless firesides up and down the county in days gone by. To get away with something like this was akin to getting away with the perfect crime, and people spoke of it for generations.

Nicholas Gosford was one such hero. He was an honest and good-natured tailor, who lived on the slopes of Pendle many years ago, but despite his virtues, he had the one great fault common to many Lancastrians: the money which he made from his cloth, and which should have supplied him and his wife with food, never seemed to get past the door of 'The Spread Eagle' at Sawley.

One evening, as he and some of his companions were sitting, pleasantly drunk, in front of the huge fire in 'The Spread Eagle', a stranger entered. He was weary of travelling, but after a tankard of the landlord's brew, he began to talk to the villagers and told them some wonderful tales. In the course of his conversation, the talk got around to the supernatural, and the stranger told how a friend of his had acquired wealth through selling his soul to the Devil. Nicholas, always short of money, latched on to the story and, after asking many questions, hit upon an idea.

The following day, while his wife was away from the home, he repeated the incantations he had learned the previous night from the stranger, laying it on thick, and to his surprise the Devil and two attendant imps very soon appeared before him. With a terrible voice, the Devil asked Nicholas what he wanted of him. Nicholas then exclaimed, "Make me rich, my Lord." The Devil said he would give him three wishes, which must be the first that either he or his wife would make after they met, and in return Nicholas must give him his soul in twenty years time. The bargain was sealed.

On the return of his wife, Nicholas demanded his tea, but she was able to give him only oatcake and butter. She said she wished she had a backstone of her own on which to do her own baking. Immediately, a backstone was placed on the fire by some invisible hand. Nicholas flew into a rage and wished it was broken in pieces. It was immediately done.

The next morning, Nicholas, on getting up, saw that he needed a shave very badly. As it was a cold morning, he said to himself, "I wish I had a can of hot water." A can was immediately placed on the table, and Nicholas, realizing that the three wishes had been granted, knew that he was as far from being rich as ever.

Time passed, and soon the day arrived for the Devil to collect the soul of Nicholas Gosford. Suddenly, with a flash of lightning the Devil appeared to claim him. Nicholas spoke harshly to him, saying he had been cheated and that the Devil had treated him meanly with the three wishes, which never did him any good. The Devil said he would allow Nicholas one final wish, advising him to wish something good for his family. Nicholas thought quickly and, seeing a horse grazing outside his door, said: "My Lord, I take thee at thy word. I wish that thou wer't riding into Hell on yonder horse, and never able to return to plague either me or any other poor mortal!" The Devil uttered a yell that was heard as far away as Colne, as an invisible power placed him on the horse and he was carried away. Afterwards, it is said that Nicholas set himself up in an inn, and thousands of people came from all parts of the world to marvel at the man who had fairly outwitted the Devil himself.

People sell their souls for many reasons — power, love, money, fame, but Lady Sybil of Bernshaw Tower had a different reason for selling hers.

Nothing remains visible of Bernshaw Tower. Odd pieces of stone from the foundations are stumbled across from time to time, but the Tower, formerly a small, fortified house, is no more. It stood five miles from Burnley, in one of the beautiful ravines which branch off from the Cliviger Gorge, quite close to the well-known 'Eagles Crag'.

Its last owner and heiress, Lady Sybil, was celebrated for her wealth and beauty, and she was also, unlike many members of her sex at that time, intellectual. She frequently visited Eagles Crag to study the flora and fauna to be found in the area and to admire the varied aspects of the surrounding countryside. The Crag had a profound effect on her, however, and on occasions she felt a great desire to possess supernatural powers.

Tradition has it that, during one of these periods, she was induced to sell her soul to the Devil in order that she might join the nightly revelries of the famous Lancashire witches. The bond was sealed and attested with her blood, and from this time on she was promised that her wishes would come true.

At that time Hapton Tower was occupied by a member of the well-known Towneley family, Lord William, who had for a long time been a suitor of Lady Sybil of Bernshaw Tower, though she constantly spurned his proposals of marriage. In utter despair, the smitten Lord William enlisted the aid of Mother Helston, a well-known Lancashire witch, who, after using many spells and much hocus-pocus, promised that he would be successful on the next All Hallows' Eve.

The following Hallowe'en Lord William went out hunting and, on nearing Eagles Crag, startled a white doe which his dogs immediately chased. Dogs and hunter chased the doe around the countryside for miles until finally, when the dogs and horses were nearing exhaustion, they again approached the Crag. Here the pack was joined by a strange hound which, according to legend, was the familiar of Mother Helston and which had been sent by her to capture the Lady Sybil, now disguised as the white doe. Just as the doe was making for a precipice, the strange hound seized her by the throat and held her fast, until Lord William threw an enchanted silken leash around her neck and led her in triumph to Hapton Tower.

During the night a fearful storm blew up, and the Tower shook as if caught in an earthquake, but on the following morning the captured doe appeared as the fair heiress of Bernshaw. With the aid of Mother Helston, counter-spells were adopted, and Lady Sybil's pact with the Devil and her powers of witchcraft were suspended. Soon she and Lord William were married, and they returned to Hapton Tower to live happily ever after.

At least, that should have been the ending, but the Devil does not give in quite as easily as this, and within a couple of years Lady Sybil was back in his power and had again taken up her supernatural practices.

While enjoying a frolic in Cliviger Mill, this time in the form of a white cat, she had one paw cut off by a manservant, who had been sent to watch by Giles Robinson, the miller. Visitors to Hapton Tower the following day found Lady Sybil at home in bed, pale and exhausted, but the presence of a manservant, bearing a lady's hand, soon solved the mystery of her sudden indisposition. By some means, known only to themselves, the hand was restored to Lady Sybil's arm, but a fine red mark around the wrist bore evidence of the sharpness of the manservant's knife. After some time, she was reconciled with her husband, but her health deteriorated rapidly from then on, and it soon became apparent that the beautiful Lady Sybil was dying.

A number of neighbouring clergy were called in and requested to exorcize the dying woman and cancel the Devil's bond. This being done, she died in peace, but after that time Bernshaw Tower remained deserted.

Tradition has it that her body was buried where the dark Eagles Crag shoots out its cold, bare peak into the sky, and on All Hallows' Eve the hound and the white doe meet a spectral huntsman in full chase.

Not all souls are given willingly to the Devil, and not all souls are collected by Satan himself. Sometimes the dead are allowed to return from the depths of Hell, on condition that the devil spirits re-enter someone else.

A storm was gathering over Rivington Pike as a small group of horsemen returned, tired and cold, after their day's hunting on the wild moors above Horwich. As the dark clouds gathered, the storm seeming to lie in their path, the men decided to shelter in a nearby tower rather than make their way to the inn as originally planned.

One member of the group, a man called Norton, seemed strangely disturbed by the storm, and the dogs, as they sheltered, began to growl and bark uneasily.

A horse's hooves were suddenly heard, as if some horseman was galloping towards the tower at great speed. Norton opened the door as the horse stopped outside, and he saw, framed against the storm-laden, moonlit sky, a horseman on a black mount. To his amazement, Norton recognized the horseman as his uncle, who had disappeared on the moors several years previously.

The strange horseman rode off, and Norton followed him. His friends wanted to follow too, but one member of the group advised against it. He told of a night several years before, when his father had gone out poaching: he had waited for his return, but only the dogs came back, alone and dirty.

When the storm abated and Norton had not come back, the party returned to the inn, hoping to find him there. However, Norton was not there, so they set out onto the moor again, to look for him.

They eventually found him at the foot of a pile of stones, which marked the spot where two shepherds had died and was known locally as 'The Two Lads'. He lay with his hands tightly clenched, looking as if he had been involved in a fearful struggle with someone or something. Norton was gently carried back to the inn, and a servant was sent running for a doctor. After he had examined the patient, the doctor stated that he was suffering from both mental and physical exhaustion.

Norton remained unconscious for several weeks. Eventually, though, he began to recover and told his friends a strange and chilling tale.

He said that the spectral horseman who had appeared at the door of the tower on the night of the storm had been his uncle, who had asked him to take him to the Two Lads. When they reached the spot, the horseman threw some of the stones high into the air, and where the stones had been, there now appeared to be nothing but a black pit. He had made Norton remain by the pit during the worst of the storm, promising to reveal the purpose of his visitation at midnight. Norton lost consciousness, and when he came to several hours later, the stones were as they had always been. At midnight, the horseman returned, saying he wished to possess the body of Norton, who was, by this time, convinced that his uncle was allowed to return only on condition that the devil spirits which possessed him re-entered someone else. He put up a brave fight, refusing to submit to his uncle.

As a result of this, the spectral horseman was never seen again, but the locals do say that if ever travellers stray too near the Two Lads late on a stormy night, they may hear the hoof-beats of the Devil's horse, racing towards the twelve-foot pile of stones.

Far fetched? Well, a spectral horseman has been seen on the moors, and certain of the events are chronicled as having taken place, although their explanation remains a mystery.

Similar mystery-shrouded chronicles surround the building of Rochdale church.

During the reign of William the Conqueror, a Saxon named Gamel decided to build himself a church on the banks of the River Roach at Rochdale. The foundations were laid and all was ready for the building to commence, when, according to legend, that night the materials were removed and found the following morning at the top of a nearby hill – an inhuman feat.

Gamel was annoyed when he heard about this and issued a proclamation saying that the guilty parties would be sought out and punished. The terrified villagers decided that it was the work not of human hands but of the heathen gods worshipped by their ancestors, whose altars they had destroyed and who were now taking their revenge. They gave a pledge to Gamel that the materials would be returned to the original site and that a watch would be kept overnight. The men were arguing among themselves as to who would stay on the first night, when a woman called 'Old Cicely' came up to them, cursing and mocking them for being cowards. Now Old Cicely had a son, who, it was said, was the result of her illicit union with the Devil. The boy was dumb, but the old woman somehow understood his mumblings. The people thought them both evil.

Finally, they offered to give the woman food and clothes if her son would keep watch during the night. After much argument, she eventually agreed.

The next morning the building had again been moved, and the boy was missing. Terrified, the men went to report to Gamel, who this time threatened to have them thrown into prison and ordered that the old woman be brought to him. Old Cicely wept and told Gamel that she had been bribed into letting her son keep watch. A man was summoned, who claimed that on the previous night he had seen the Devil at work, moving the church. Gamel did not believe this story until a stranger reported seeing phantom beings moving loads, far heavier than a normal man could move. Not knowing them to be the Devil's helpers, he had gone to their assistance, and they had given him a silver ring as a reward for his labour.

Suddenly, a shout was heard from the courtyard, and Cicely's son appeared. Seeing the silver ring, he gave a hideous shout and, grabbing it off the man, placed it on his own finger. At once he appeared to grow more evil-looking. Gamel screamed at his guards to seize him, but the boy fled, and when the guards reached the battlements, only a thin wisp of smoke was to be seen, far below in the valley. Gamel decided that there was nothing for it but to build his new church on a different site to please the Devil. This was done, and that is why the church stands at the top of the hill, reached by 124 steps.

The Devil is also said to have interfered with the building of Burnley Parish Church and Winwick Church.

Godly Lane Cross stood in a small plantation a few hundred yards from the original old market-place of Burnley. It was recorded as being of 'great antiquity' and had most probably been moved from the churchyard to the site. It was thought to be a Saxon relic and, like those at Whalley and Dewsbury, to commemorate the preaching of Paulinus, the first Christian missionary in these parts, about AD 597.

Tradition has it that, prior to the foundation of any church in Burnley, pagan rites were celebrated on the spot where the cross stood. When work was started on the building of a church on that spot, the materials were removed each night by the Devil's imps, who came in the form of pigs and carried the materials to the spot where the present St Peter's Church now stands.

Winwick Church is surrounded by a similar legend. Its foundation was laid where the founder had directed, and the close of the first day's labour showed that the workmen had not been idle. At dusk a pig was seen running hastily on the site of the new church, and as he ran, he was heard to cry and scream, "Wee-ee-wick, wee-ee-wick, wee-ee-wick". Then, taking a stone in his mouth, he carried it to a spot said to have been sanctified by St Oswald.

There are other churches in Lancashire whose sites have been changed by the Devil and he has also had a hand in building bridges: that at Kirkby Lonsdale owes much of its beauty to the string of his apron giving way, when he was carrying stones in it. According to some, it was the Devil who stamped his foot into the church wall at Brindle, to prove the truth about 'Popery' – much as George Marsh did at Smithills Hall, to prove the truth about Protestantism.

Nearly all the stories about the Devil and his works are of a similar nature, one story doing for several places, except that at Winwick and

Burnley he appeared as a pig, at Leyland as a cat and somewhere else as a fish.

The Devil is, of course, known to appear in different guises, in order to obtain the soul of the unwary. For instance he is said to have appeared in the guise of a mermaid to an eighteenth-century sailor on the Black Rock, which is situated in the Mersey estuary. The sailor, returning from a long voyage, saw the beautiful mermaid sitting upon a rock, combing her long golden hair, and fell in love with her instantly. The mermaid returned his love and gave him her ring, promising that they would soon be re-united. Five days later the sailor died, but he is said to appear now and again on the Black Rock, trying to warn other sailors of the fate that awaits them.

A similar story of an encounter with the Devil in disguise is told further north, around Fair Snape Fell.

One fine night, a young man by the name of Giles Roper was returning home across Fair Snape Fell when he came to a spot which was reputed to be haunted by the Devil himself. However, the vision which appeared to Giles was not of a horned head and cloven hooves but of a tall, slender girl in white, with lovely golden hair, sitting on some rocks. She was, to his mind, beautiful, the loveliest creature he had ever seen, far more beautiful than the miller's daughter, to whom he was engaged to be married, and he fell instantly in love with her.

The golden-haired girl beckoned him in a most provocative manner, bidding him to come to her. Being a full-blooded Lancashire lad, he needed no second invitation and was within a few feet of her when she mysteriously vanished and he found himself alone, but for the gaunt black rocks where the girl had been sitting. He went back home, still madly in love with the beautiful apparition.

The following night, instead of courting the miller's daughter as he had arranged, he went to the Fell in the hope of seeing the lovely phantom that had so enchanted him. He was not disappointed. She was sitting on the same rock and, on seeing him, she smilingly held out her white arms to greet him. Again, as he approached her, she suddenly vanished. He went home more infatuated than at his first meeting.

Now, the miller's daughter, a full-blooded Lancashire lass, was, to say the least, annoyed at poor Giles for missing his date on the previous night and tackled him about it, insisting that he give her a good explanation. Naturally, when he told her he had been up to the Fell to see the beautiful ghost, she did not believe it and paid some men to follow Giles if he should go up there again.

They followed him up to the Fell the following night and saw him hold out his hands and run to some invisible being on the rocks. When they returned and told the miller's daughter what they had seen, she felt relieved – but at the same time worried about her future husband's sanity.

Seeing Giles the following day, she joked with him about the ghost and tried to persuade him to visit her as usual instead of going to the Fell. Her pleading, however, went unheeded. His infatuation for the beautiful ghost increased. He continued to visit the Fell night after night, until he became so ill that he eventually had to be taken to his bed. In his delirium he kept appealing to the spirit with the golden hair to come to him and love him.

Before he was fully recovered from his illness, he got up from his bed one cold, misty night and made his way quietly out of the house. He was found on the Fell the following morning, lying on the ground in front of the haunted boulder, dead and with the look of the most frightened horror on his face. In the soft soil which surrounded his body were several imprints – the imprints of cloven hooves!

13

GREY LADIES

Lancashire abounds with grey ladies who, although long dead, seem to be some of the commonest kinds of wraiths. Many of our old houses and mansions are reputed to be haunted by some former mistress who met with a tragic end. Many stories are no doubt true and have been well authenticated many times, while others leave us in some doubt.

But these old houses do have atmospheres, and whether they be in ruins or are complete, with long passages, oak-panelled rooms and the like, it is not surprising that they acquire a ghost. The rest is left to the imagination, which in many instances needs little encouragement.

The Norris family lived at Speke Hall, near Liverpool, for over five centuries, providing the country with soldiers and statesmen. They also gave the Hall a haunted room, a ghostly apparition and an empty cradle which is rocked, even today, by invisible hands.

In Tudor times the Norrises were very active in demolishing and rebuilding, the present Hall (little of which is changed today) being completed during the reign of Henry VIII. Like most of their neighbours, they refused to change their religion during the period of persecution of Catholics under the Tudors, and in spite of great pressures being brought to bear, they remained strong in their faith. Because of its position at Speke, with the nearby ford across the River Mersey, the Hall became an active Mass-centre and a reception- and departure-point for priests and Catholics fleeing for their lives. The Hall is riddled with hides and secret rooms, which were well-used during the Elizabethan era. The panelled walls conceal hidden chambers, and escape-passages run all around the Hall.

During the reign of the Catholic Queen Mary and later under James I, the Norrises received many royal favours, which they returned by supporting Charles I in the Civil War. The last of the male line of the Norrises died after the Restoration, leaving as sole heir his daughter Mary who had married one Lord Sidney Beauclerk, a self-styled literary gentleman and patron of the arts, who counted among his friends Samuel Johnson and Sir Joshua Reynolds. Beauclerk was not a very good husband, however, and he caused Mary so much unhappiness that she is said to have ended her life and that of her son Topham by throwing herself, child in her arms, into the moat.

It is thought to be poor Mary's ghost which now haunts the Hall and her hands which still rock the child's cradle quite regularly, all these centuries later.

There is, however, some doubt about the identity of the Speke Hall ghost, for it is thought to be unlikely that the Beauclerks actually lived here. But there is no doubt that one of the rooms, the tapestry room, is haunted, as quite a number of people have felt a presence here. The cradle has been seen rocking, and an apparition has been seen in one of the bedrooms, where it disappears through a wall near the window. Recent examination has brought to light a concealed entrance to a passage, leading down through an outside wall.

Not many miles away, in the flat countryside about seven miles from Ormskirk, stands Rufford Old Hall, a fifteenth-century manor house believed to have replaced an older house and which has been altered twice since the days of Robert Hesketh, who held the Manor until 1490. Now the Hall comprises the original Great Hall of timber construction, a brick wing, added about 1660, and an intervening section dating from the early-nineteenth century. It was presented to the National Trust by the late Lord Hesketh in 1936, along with land to preserve the surroundings, plus an endowment fund.

Tradition has it that the young William Shakespeare once performed at the Hall. Indeed, there is evidence that one 'William Shakeshaft' was a member of the Hesketh players who visited Rufford around 1584. This does, in fact, coincide with Shakespeare's absence from home after stealing deer in Charlecote Park.

Like most families in the area, the Heskeths were Catholics, and their beliefs were to cause them quite a lot of grief during the persecution. Priests were harboured at Rufford, and above a canopy in the Great Hall, a secret chamber is concealed, part of its clay floor remaining in position. This chamber was discovered only in 1949, but it is believed to have been constructed during the religious strife in the second half of the sixteenth century.

There is a well-authenticated ghost of a lady in grey at the Hall, who has been seen quite often and quite clearly in the grounds, her form solid-looking, though she is said to cast no shadow. This grey lady is thought by many to be the ghost of a member of the Hesketh family whose husband was called away to some Scottish war soon after their wedding. Some time later, she was told by a soldier passing through the village that her husband was on his way back home. In vain the poor girl waited, but her husband never came. She refused her food and in time was taken to her bed, where her condition gradually deteriorated and she died. It is said that, on her death-bed the poor girl promised that her spirit would stay on at the Hall to await her lover's return.

Another ghost, said to be that of Queen Elizabeth I, has also been reported seen in the dining-room on at least two occasions. However, as there is no record of the Queen's ever staying at the Hall, this ghost cannot really be authenticated. Still, who knows? She is always said to be popping up in some remote country house or another.

Yet another grey lady pops up in the village of Croston, just a few miles away.

On the A581, about six miles west of Chorley, stands Croston Farm, which until recently housed what was known as 'the Royal Umpire Exhibition'. The museum, alas no more, took its name from its prize exhibit, the famous Royal Liverpool Umpire stagecoach, which ran from Liverpool to London about 150 years ago. The museum housed, in its day, some of the finest horse-drawn vehicles in the country including the postillion carriage which Queen Victoria used when she visited Lord Derby at Knowsley.

The farmhouse itself goes back many centuries and was originally the home of the Gradwell family of Croston. Again, the family were devout Roman Catholics, and several of its members went into the priesthood. During the persecution, many priests are known to have found a safe refuge here. Indeed, in the garden is a stone cross which commemorates one of these priests, the chaplain of the Gradwell family, Father Winkley.

The house has been haunted for several centuries by a ghost familiarly known as 'The Sarscowe Lady', who used to be heard stepping down the old oak stairway, her rustling skirt sweeping the treads. Legend has it that the ghost is that of a girl who was deeply in love with Father Winkley and who lived at nearby Sarscowe Farm. It is said she caught a fever and, in her tormented and delirious state, plunged to her death down a deep well behind the house.

Round about 1958, the stone cross memorial to Father Winkley was removed from its original site in the orchard and set up in the garden, since when the ghostly visitations appear to have ceased, although a strange thing occurred on the very day the cross was removed: several hours afterwards a bus stopped at the end of the drive, and the bus-driver refused to go any further, saying that he was sure he had run over a woman. Was it the Sarscowe Lady walking again?

Over the years there have been reports of sightings of a slim, white girl and of many strange noises, including the sounds of moving furniture and footsteps on an upstairs landing. An apparition is said to have appeared from under a stone by the great hearth, where a hide had been constructed with an escape-route to Croston Church. Was this the usual mode of entry for the Sarscowe Lady for her clandestine meetings with Father Winkley?

Next to the farmhouse stands a barn where unexplained phenomena have been reported quite recently. Showers of stones and the sound of heavy, strenuous breathing and other mysterious noises have been heard in this building, which many years ago was a church.

Another grey lady who causes trouble with passing bus-drivers can be met on the A677, just about half way between Preston and Blackburn at the old Samlesbury Hall, which was built during the reign of Edward III, oak from the surrounding primeval forests being selected for the massive timbers which form the framework for this lovely old building.

In the reign of Henry II, Gospatrick de Samlesbury took his seat in the nearby predecessor of the present Hall. In or about the middle of the thirteenth century, the heiress Cecily de Samlesbury married John de Ewyes, who died without a male heir, so the Hall passed to their daughter, who was married to Sir Gilbert de Southworth, in whose family the Hall remained for more than 350 years.

It is with Sir John Southworth, who died in 1595, that our story begins. Before his death, one of his daughters, Dorothy, fell in love with the heir of a neighbouring knightly, but Protestant, house. Sir John was enraged that his daughter should even contemplate marrying the son of a family which had deserted the Catholic faith, and he forbade the youth to come anywhere near her again. The old adage about true love not running smoothly applied in those days too, and Sir John's wrath only served to make the young couple more determined to marry. After many secret meetings, the couple agreed to elope, but unfortunately the time and place were overheard by one of the girl's brothers, who was hiding in the bushes nearby and who determined to prevent what he considered to be his sister's disgrace.

On the night the couple had planned to elope, they met at the pre-arranged hour, and, as the knight moved away with his bride-to-be, her brother rushed from his hiding-place and slew him, and two friends who were helping them. Their bodies were secretly buried near the domestic chapel at the Hall, and Lady Dorothy was sent abroad to a convent, where she is said to have gone mad and, not long after, died.

At some time during the last century, three skeletons were found near the walls of the Hall, which have helped to strengthen the tradition ever since.

On still, clear evenings, the ghost of a lady in white can be seen, passing along the corridors and gallery, then out into the grounds. There she meets a handsome knight, and together they go for a walk. They have been seen many times on the road, where, when they reach a certain spot, probably near where the lover is thought to have been buried, both ghosts stand still and embrace each other before fading away with a sigh. Weeping and wailing have also been heard, as if someone is crying bitterly.

About thirty years ago, when a play telling of the tragedy of the Southworth family was staged in the Great Hall, a member of the cast saw a lady in white passing across the garden: no member of the cast had left the Hall during this time. During the war, two soldiers met the white lady as they returned one night to their hut in the grounds, and I have heard of one caretaker's daughter who told of waking one night to find someone leaning over her bed; another woman has seen a lady in white passing along the corridors. Some people have sat all night to watch for her, and although the ghost was not seen, they heard weeping and the rustling of skirts and saw a chair rocking of its own accord. More recently, a bus passing on the main road to Blackburn actually stopped for her, the driver taking her for a late-night passenger.

There is a mystery surrounding the ghost, however. The only Dorothy in the Southworth family of Tudor times appears to have been a sister of Sir John and, by all accounts, died of nothing more dramatic than 'natural causes'. But there is a ghost – that cannot be denied, for it has been seen and authenticated by dozens of people over the years. Whether it is the ghost of Lady Dorothy is open to conjecture.

The old Hall is also associated with Grace Sowerbutts, a local and notorious witch, who was tried and acquitted of witchcraft, while her colleagues paid for their crimes with the full severity of the law. Is it any wonder, then, that for years after the notorious witch-trials of the seventeenth century, stories of boggarts, hell hounds and other spectres made this a place to be avoided, even by the hardiest of locals. Even today, driving from the M6 towards Blackburn late at night gives one an uncomfortable feeling.

Another tragic ghost of one who died for love can be met around Christmas-time at Dunkenhalgh Park, Clayton-le-Moors, about five miles west of Burnley.

Dunkenhalgh was an estate on which Judge Sir Thomas Walmesley spent a small fortune in building and enlarging in the seventeenth century. The grounds of the house stretched for miles, and there were over six hundred acres of deer-park enclosed in them. The family home is now the Dunkenhalgh Hotel, an old English residential hotel, well known for its cuisine.

In the early part of the eighteenth century, the sixteen-year-old great-grand-daughter of old Sir Thomas married one Robert Petre, and they moved into the family home at Dunkenhalgh Park. Children were born, and, to take care of them, they took on a succession of nannies and governesses, one of whom was a pretty young French girl called Lucette, who loved the children and was in turn loved by them: she laughed and played with them and listened to their problems. She was also adored by most other members of the Petre household and by everyone with whom she came into contact.

Lucette would take the children on long walks through the grounds, often giving lessons under the trees in the deer park. One of their favourite spots was down by the old bridge which spans the River Hindburn, where her ghost can be encountered to this day.

It appears that the governess had a love-affair with a young army officer from the neighbourhood, who had just returned from the wars in Europe. He was from an old Dunkenhalgh family, a handsome, gay and debonair lad who was home for Christmas. Lucette found his flattery and charm irresistible and fell madly in love with him. He found her good looks and laughing eyes enchanting and returned her love. Soon, however, he was obliged to rejoin his unit, but before he did so, he vowed his love to Lucette and promised to marry her on his return, probably in the spring.

But spring came and went without any sign of the young officer's returning. By the summer Lucette was not only in despair but also seven months pregnant. The Petre family were, of course, understanding and took good care of the girl, but the gossiping and whispering of the below-stairs staff put an unbearable strain on her. She longed to return to her family in France, but, as her parents were strict, she dared not do so.

At the height of a summer storm, when the waters of the river were swollen, she threw herself from the old bridge and ended her short, tragic life. Her body was found downstream the following morning, floating face down among the reeds. Gently she was lifted from the water, wrapped in a shroud and carried back to the big house.

The irony of all this is that the young officer returned only a week or two after the unfortunate girl took her life, unaware of the tragedy that had taken place.

Lucette's brother also arrived, having hurried over from France on hearing the sad news. He met up with the young officer, accused him of being responsible for his sister's death and challenged him to a duel. The saddened officer had no heart for a fight, but, being both a gentleman and an officer in the army of King George, he would have been branded a coward if he had refused. Although the soldier was the better swordsman, he was mortally wounded in the duel, by a savage thrust of the Frenchman's rapier.

Now, around Christmas-time, Lucette's ghost can be seen, dressed in a shroud, drifting silently among the trees, walking by the river and disappearing at the old stone bridge, at the spot where she threw herself into the turbulent waters over two hundred years ago.

Lytham Hall, built by Cuthbert Clifton of Westby in 1610, is said to be haunted by a 'white lady'. The house was partly demolished by fire

Wycoller Hall, legendary site of the spectral horseman. The ghost of a woman in black has been seen here occasionally, but no one can claim to have seen the horseman.

Towneley Hall, Burnley. The grounds are said to be the haunt of Sir John Towneley, who haunts the acres full of remorse and who demands a life every seven years.

in about 1745, and the new Georgian frontage was designed by John Carr, making it one of the most beautiful Halls in the county. The older portion of the Hall, not affected by the fire, has been converted to offices now but for many years remained as it had been when the house was first built. The long gallery belongs to this period, as do the domestic chapel and the old servants' quarters.

It is in the long gallery that many people, including nurses and convalescing servicemen who were housed there during the last war, claim to have seen the 'white lady' drifting along the gallery and fading away at the far end.

The Scarlet Room at Heskin Hall near Blackburn is reputed to be haunted by another 'white lady'.

In Tudor times this manor belonged to the Molyneux family and then to the Mawdesleys, great landowners. However, although the house saw much suffering by both families during the Tudor period, this particular ghost is thought to hark back to the Civil War: according to tradition, it is that of a young girl who lived at the Hall during that period.

It is a well-documented fact that Cromwell showed little mercy to the Catholic Lancastrians, and when Roundhead soldiers raided Heskin Hall, they flushed out a terrified priest, who disclaimed his religion, screaming his devotion to the Puritan faith, and, to prove his point, seized the Catholic daughter of the house and offered to hang her. It is thought that the priest carried out his threat and hanged the girl in front of her parents, either from a beam in the kitchen or in the Scarlet Room, where she is often seen today. Strange tappings and bangings are heard from time to time, and the atmosphere in the Scarlet Room always gives one the feeling of oppression.

At Bolton-le-Sands, three miles north of Morecambe, the canal bank is haunted by the spectre of a local woman who was drowned in the canal several years ago.

Finally, we find the ghost which serves as a reminder of the age when ten years of widowhood was not thought sufficient expiation of the crime of taking a second husband.

Standing in front of a school in Standishgate, Wigan, is the base and stump of an old cross, which is said to forever perpetuate the memory of the medieval Lady Mabel Bradshaigh of Haigh Hall, which stands two or three miles away. She was the daugher and sole heiress of Hugh Norris de Haigh and Blackrod, and her husband, Sir William Bradshaigh, second son of Sir John, was a great traveller and soldier.

Tradition has it that Sir William went off to fight in the Holy Wars and remained away for nearly ten years – in actual fact, Sir William was not born until ten years after the sixth and final Crusade and probably fought in the campaign of Edward II against the Scots, which ended in disaster for Edward. Sir William's long absence from home is accounted for by the fact that he was probably captured and spent the greater part of his absence as a hostage in some Scottish castle. During his absence, his wife, quite naturally, presumed him dead, and she married a Welsh knight.

One day, the sad Lady Mabel, whose second marriage was an unhappy one, was distributing charity to the poor of Haigh, when she saw in the crowd a palmer (pilgrim) whose features bore a striking resemblance to those of her former husband. On seeing this face from the past she wept and returned to Haigh Hall, where her Welsh husband is said to have chastised her.

She had not been mistaken. The palmer was indeed her long-lost husband, who had donned the disguise and mingled with the crowds to avoid embarrassment. Seeing his lady's distress, however, he made himself known to his tenants and, hearing of the usurper's villainy, set out after the Welsh knight, who by this time had been warned and was starting out on a hasty flight south. Sir William overtook him at Newton-le-Willows and in the ensuing fight slew the villain.

Sir William and Lady Mabel were now happily re-united. She, however, was obliged by her confessor to walk once every week, dressed in penitential attire, bare-footed and bare-legged, from the chapel at Haigh Hall to the spot where the cross now stands, a distance of about two miles. This cross has subsequently become known as 'Mab's Cross'.

Sir William was outlawed for a year and a day for killing the Welsh knight, but it is said that he and his wife lived happily until their deaths. They were buried in the Parish Church of All Saints at Wigan, where the remains of the effigies on their tomb have now been decayed by time, though it is still possible to make out the figure of a knight in a coat of mail, cross-legged and with his sword partly drawn from the scabbard by his left side. Beside him lies his lady, dressed in a long robe, her hands elevated and joined, as if in fervent prayer.

Local people claim that from time to time a shadowy figure, dressed in ragged clothing, bare-footed and bare-legged, has been seen making its way along the route taken by Lady Mabel during her weekly penance.

14

DARK MYSTERIOUS GENTLEMEN

For every grey lady in the county, there is a spectral male counterpart. The story behind some of these ghosts may not be as romantic but they are equally as tragic in many instances. Many are the result of the religious persecutions of the sixteenth century and of the Civil War, while others result from some foul deed committed in the course of some long-forgotten cause. Some, like the phantom at the Castle de Burgh, are just as a result of unhappiness, the reason for which is lost in time.

Castle de Burgh was an ancient structure in the city of Liverpool, originally the property of the de Burgh family. Well over 150 years ago, the last member of the de Burgh family died, and the castle was let to various tenants, one of whom was a carpenter.

One night, the carpenter was working late at his shop, a few hundred yards from the castle, with four or five of his men. Glancing up from his work, he saw, to his surprise, a gentleman in mourning-clothes pass by his bench. At once the poor carpenter was struck by a violent fit of trembling; his hair stood on end, and he broke out into a cold sweat. Suddenly, every gas-light in the workshop went out of its own accord, and the men, now thoroughly frightened, hurriedly left for their respective homes.

On arriving home at the castle, the carpenter climbed the staircase to his room, and, as he did so, he heard footsteps behind him. Turning round, he was horrified to see the same gentleman in mourning-clothes. Terrified, the carpenter bounded up the remaining stairs to his room and at once barred and bolted the door, leaning his head against it to regain his breath. Looking around, his heart missed a beat, for standing before the fireplace was the same apparition. The poor carpenter passed out from sheer terror.

The ghost was seen regularly after that by a number of people, who swore it was the ghost of the last member of the de Burgh family. A local priest is said to have been called in, and on one occasion the ghost told him that it was not happy – presumably because the old castle had been converted after his death. The castle stands no longer, alas, and as far as I know, the ghost has not been seen in the vicinity for well over a century.

Wycoller Hall, near Colne, is best-known as the setting for 'Fearndean Manor' in Charlotte Brontë's novel *Jane Eyre*. It was long the home of the Cunliffes of Billington, who were noted personages in their day – the names of successive members of the family are attached to documents relating to the property of the abbots of Whalley.

In the days of the Commonwealth, the loyalty of the Cunliffes to the Crown cost them dearly. Their ancestral estates at Billington were seized, and they returned to Wycoller. About 1820, the last of the family died, and the Hall was allowed to decline and become the ruins which are left standing today. The room spoken about in the legend no longer remains, and one is not able to identify the part of the Hall in which it was situated, only the beautiful, large stone fireplace and the stone stairs leading over it remain in one piece, a target for vandals.

Tradition has it that once every year Wycoller Hall is visited by a spectral horseman dressed in the costume of the late-Tudor or early-Stuart period. On the evening of his visit, the weather is always wild with no moon to light the road. When the howling wind is at its loudest, the horseman can be heard galloping up the road at full speed and, after crossing the narrow bridge, comes to a sudden halt at the door of the Hall. The rider then dismounts and makes his way into the Hall. Dreadful screams are heard, which in time turn to moans. The horseman then re-appears at the door, mounts his horse and gallops off in the direction from which he came.

The basis of this haunting is that one of the Cunliffes murdered his wife in an upstairs bedroom, and the spectral horseman is the ghost of the murderer. His victim is said to have predicted the extinction of the family – a prediction which has now been fulfilled.

My favourite version is that the phantom horseman is the ghost of Simon Cunliffe, Squire of Wycoller, who, it is said, sounds his hunting-horn when a tragedy is imminent. This version tells how he was out hunting one day when the fox tried to take refuge in the Hall itself, running up the stairs. Simon, following the creature in hot pursuit, rode up the wide staircase and into his wife's room, causing her to collapse and die of shock. I am told that before the staircase was removed, hoofmarks could be seen quite plainly on two of the stairs, although I doubt if they were in anyway connected with this legend.

No one can claim to have seen this spectral horseman, but another ghost has been seen at the vicinity of the Hall, the ghost of a woman dressed in black and reputed to be the wife of the spectral horseman. Another theory, probably more correct, is that she was the wife of one of the Cunliffes who was drowned at sea in the seventeenth century and who appears from time to time in search of her husband.

Although Towneley Hall, near Burnley, is not itself haunted, there is a ghost which roams the old Towneley lands full of remorse.

The story of the remarkable Towneley family has been written many times, by people better qualified than I. Let me just say that the family history goes far beyond any written memorial: they were staunch to both the Crown and the Catholic Church, and no family has suffered more for the sake of loyalty than this one.

Generations of Towneleys distinguished themselves in warfare: a Richard Towneley fought at Agincourt with a band of local men in 1415; Charles Towneley, born in 1600, was a supporter of Charles I and bled to death at the Battle of Marston Moor; his son Richard engaged in the plot to restore James II; his grandson, another Richard, joined the Jacobite rebels in 1715, was caught and tried at Preston, but was acquitted; the second Richard's brother Francis joined the company supporting Bonnie Prince Charlie in the '45 rebellion and was executed after the Battle of Carlisle in 1746; Sir John Towneley escaped from Culloden, serving the same cause, and escaped to France.

Our story concerns the medieval John Towneley (1473–1541), who was knighted on the battlefield in Scotland and became Sheriff of Lancashire in 1531. In 1490 the King gave permission for the Towneley estate to be emparked, and in 1514 John was granted permission to enclose his estates at Hapton. In doing so, he caused considerable hardship to the country folk by dispossessing them of their ancient rights of common, and on occasion he resorted to having them thrown out of their homes bodily. A band of hired rough-necks then proceeded to destroy the meagre cottages. This ruthlessness enriched Sir John's estate by a further two hundred acres and caused much bitterness and suffering among the poor folk, the memory of which is alleged to have tormented him for the rest of his life. After he died, his ghost roamed the Hall and the disputed acres, wailing, as if in remorse, for the dark deeds committed in the early years of the sixteenth century. He is said to materialize every seven years, crying piteously:

Be warned, lay out! Be warned, lay out!
Around Horelaw and Hollinhey Clough.
To her children give back the widow's cot,
For you and yours there is more than enough!

It is also said that the spirit demanded one life every seven years and that some fatal accident happened at the end of each period.

The origin of Osbaldeston Hall, near Ribchester, goes back to the time of the Saxons. Presumably it was the home of Oswald, this being another form of the name, a *ton* being the home or estate. In the twelfth century we find Eilfi of Osbaldeston, a Saxon who had a son whose name appears in documents about 1240. The property remained with the family until the death of Thomas, son of Edward Osbaldeston, the last male heir of the line, in about 1700.

The Hall at Osbaldeston is, alas, a reduced structure, forming part of a farm, but from old documents and plans one can see that it was a house of some size originally consisting of two wings and a larger central portion set further back. The large drawing-room contained a fireplace, over which were some very elaborate carvings, containing the family coats-of-arms.

According to a number of ancients living in the area, there used to be one room in the Hall in which the walls were smeared with several reddish-brown marks, which, it was said, could never be erased. Tradition has it that they were made by blood when one of the family was murdered, some time towards the end of the seventeenth century.

Once, so the story goes, there had been a large family gathering at the Hall. After the lavish meal was over, the wine began to flow in earnest, and, as a result, some trifling family argument began. Before long, what began as an argument ended as a tragedy, when Thomas Osbaldeston challenged his brother-in-law to a duel. Other members of the family, seeing the argument turning into something more sinister, interfered, and soon Thomas appeared to quieten down. Not so. Soon afterwards the two men met in this room, supposedly by accident, and Thomas Osbaldeston drew his sword and treacherously murdered his brother-in-law, who offered little or no resistance, for which crime, Thomas forfeited his lands. Ever since that time the room had been haunted by the ghost of the murdered man, who continued to visit the scene of the crime. During the silent hours of the night, the ghost could be seen passing from room to room with uplifted arms and with the appearance of blood coming from severe jagged chest-wounds.

A dastardly deed is also responsible for the ghost which haunts the site of Lostock Tower, which lay about four miles to the west of Bolton. It was originally an imposing structure by all accounts, built mainly from wood and plaster and surrounded by a moat.

The Tower formerly belonged to the Andertons but, in the early nineteenth century, came into the possession of the Blundells of Ince. There is a story which has now passed into folk-lore, connected with the Andertons and also concerned a family called Heaton, who lived in or around the Bolton area at that time (possibly the ancestors of the present Heatons of St Helens).

The story goes that one of the Heatons was a spendthrift who fell deeply in debt and mortgaged his manor and lands to Anderton of the Tower. When the day arrived for the mortgage to be paid, the Heatons had not quite raised the amount of capital to pay it off and so did not arrive to settle up. The day wore on, and quite early in the evening, the Andertons retired to bed. Not long afterwards, however, the Heatons were hammering on the doors, shouting that they had at last raised the money and were ready to pay off the mortgage. Anderton had hoped they would be unable to pay, as he had designs on the property, so he refused to let them in, because, he said, they should have been ready to pay before sunset. The following morning he sent a message saying that they were too late and that he would foreclose on the mortgage. This wrong done to the Heatons was never forgiven, for now the family were utterly ruined.

It is said that the ghost of the wrong-doer is doomed to revisit the scene of his crime until the property is restored to its rightful owners. I am told that, while ever the Tower was held by the Andertons, none of their horses could ever be forced to cross the stream onto the property they had illegally acquired from the Heatons.

The ghost of Anderton is still reputed to be roaming the area of the scene of the crime, but to my knowledge it has not been seen by anyone alive today. In fact, most people have forgotten the treachery of the Andertons – that is, except perhaps for members of the Heaton family.

Much of the credit for the ability to spin fine cotton in Lancashire must inevitably go to Bolton's famous son Samuel Crompton, who lived in the picturesque fifteenth-century, half-timbered manor house known as 'Hall i' th'Wood', where he invented his famous 'mule'. This old house is haunted by the ghost of a Cavalier, who, over the years, usually at Christmas-time, has been seen to run up the wide staircase. It is thought to be the ghost of a member of the Brownlow family who built the Hall, who returned at some time during the Civil War to retrieve some incriminating evidence.

Since the ghost was only seen to go up the stairs and not return, it is thought that, whoever he was, the Cavalier must have been caught and killed in one of the upstairs rooms.

In recent years the ghost has not been seen, but his frantic footsteps have been heard only recently, racing up the staircase.

On the bank of the River Irwell at Kersal stands the seventeenth-century Kersal Cell, once the home of John Byrom and where he wrote the hymn 'Christians Awake'.

The house is an interesting, partly-timbered building, which was previously a religious house attached to Zenton Priory. At one time it fell into a ruinous condition, but it was saved from demolition by the timely efforts of the local people, who subscribed to a fund for its restoration. Subsequently, it was bought in 1951 and transformed into a private club.

There is a legend attached to Kersal Cell which goes back to the time of the Crusades, in which the head of Clayton Hall, Sir Hugh de Biron, took part. Sir Hugh was not only renowned for his mastery of arms but also the kindest of masters and the most loving of husbands, so on the day he left Clayton Hall to join the fight against the Turks, the servants wept, the dogs whined and pulled at their leashes, his tenants sadly lined the route out of the drive, and Lady Biron stood white and silent as if she knew that she was seeing her husband for the last time.

The Crusades lasted many years, and Sir Hugh was always to be found where the fighting was fiercest, gaining admiration for his skill in battle not only from his fellow warriors but from the enemy also. However, no matter how enthusiastic the warrior, one can always have too much of fighting, as of a good thing: eventually it caught up with Sir Hugh, and a great change came over him.

One day, after a fierce and bloody battle in which he had accounted for many of the enemy, he returned in the early evening to his tent. Looking around him in the gathering dusk at the dead and wounded of both sides, he suddenly became weary of the whole bloody business of war. Falling to his knees, he vowed, at the very edge of the battlefield, that never again would he lift his sword against man. Then, without a word, to anyone, he sought his horse, mounted up and rode off through the night to find the coast and take a ship back to England.

After a long, wearisome sea-voyage, the gallant knight finally reached the shores of England and on landing immediately mounted his horse and rode, post-haste, for Clayton Hall, which he reached a few days later. As he approached, he heard, drifting across the darkening meadows, the sound of melancholy chanting. Spurring his tired steed, he soon came to within sight of the Hall and saw, coming from the main door, a procession of monks carrying crosses and candlesticks. Behind them came four dark figures bearing a coffin, followed by the mourning servants and tenants of the Clayton Hall estates. Sir Hugh had arrived home too late: he was just in time to witness the funeral of his wife. He saw in her death a punishment for the suffering he himself had caused and vowed that, from that moment on, not only would he cease to be a soldier but he would enter into the service of God and serve his fellow man. He retired, according to tradition, to a little place known as 'Kersal Cell', and there he lived as a hermit for the rest of his life, praying, healing and carrying out the work of God. After his death a religious house was built on the spot.

Kersal Cell is reputed to be haunted by a monk, greyish in appearance, who wanders about the old rooms, usually at Christmas and New Year, and who is thought to be the ghost of Sir Hugh de Biron, haunting the site of the original building of over eight hundred years ago.

Another, more recent warrior haunted the St Michaels-on-Wyre district in the latter half of the nineteenth century.

Sir Ralph Longworth was an old soldier who, after a lifetime of fighting for the Royalist armies, could never rest peacefully in his grave. He fought at Preston, at Wigan Lane and finally, as a white-haired major, in Colonel Kirkby's militia. The old Hall at St Michaels-on-Wyre, where he lived, was haunted by this old boy until it was demolished in the 1860s. Apart from moving the furniture, clattering the pots and pans and banging doors, he was seen parading in the lane outside the Hall. However, there have been no reports of the ghostly major since the vicar of the parish and the parish priest performed a combined exorcism.

15

THE LANCASHIRE WITCHES

On the side of the tower of St Mary's Church, Newchurch-in-Pendle, there is the carving of an eye, said to represent the All-Seeing Eye of God. Its original function was to protect the church and the worshippers from the witches who once plagued the area. Outside the doorway to this old church, built around 1540, is a tomb supposedly of one of the witches, Alice Nutter, the richest of the Pendle witches, who lived at nearby Roughlee Hall.

Witchcraft is still taken seriously in this part of Lancashire, even today. In Barley there is a field which is reputed to have been frequented by 'Demdike's brood', and one corner of the field is to this day never cultivated because the locals consider it to be poisoned. There is a haunted barn at Huntroyd, where a man is said to have committed suicide because he thought he had been bewitched; and in Trawden people tell of bewitched cattle dancing in the shippon and of calves running wild, trying to climb the walls of their pen, on certain nights of the year. Browse through Samlesbury churchyard and you will stumble across a worn gravestone with iron spikes driven through it by the locals, because they suspected the poor woman lying there of being a witch and did not want her rising up again and haunting them.

During Tudor and Stuart times, belief in the power of evil spirits to work harm on man and beast was a very real thing. Ordinary people were inclined to attribute every sudden death, misfortune or other unusual occurrence to witches or the Devil, or to the malevolent evil spirits who worked their ill-deeds without the help of mortal witches. Even King James I had a deep-rooted fear of witchcraft: he passed a law in which "the punishment for the practice of wicked arts was death", and in 1597 he wrote his famous book *Demonology*, circulated throughout England in 1603, in which he describes the terrifying powers of the witches. The influence of this book on witchcraft led ultimately to witch-trials in many parts of the country, among the most famous of which were those which began at Lancaster Assize Courts in August 1612 and which culminated in three generations of witches being marched through the streets of Lancaster and hanged before a large crowd on the gallows at Lancaster Moor, on Thursday, 20th August 1612.

This brood is often referred to as 'the Pendle witches', because they came from the Forest of Pendle, around Pendle Hill. However, although the Pendle witches are renowned throughout the country, thanks to Harrison Ainsworth's fascinating novel, the county boasted other witches: Grace Sowerbutts of Samlesbury, Marjory Hilton of Catforth and Widow Lomeshay of Burnley, who was buried at St Peter's Church, Burnley, on 12th March 1612, just before the first enquiry into the actions of the Pendle witches was held.

There were two groups of Pendle witches. The first, the best-known of the groups that have captured the imagination, were Old Demdike and Old Chattox, two poor and decrepit old women who were both over eighty years old and who were so terrified during their examination that they were prepared to admit anything. Each accused the other and added details to their imaginary crimes.

The Clerk of the Court at Lancaster was one Thomas Potts who, after the event, wrote a book, *A Wonderfulle Discoverie of Witches in the County of Lancaster*, which not only tells of the trials and confessions of the witches but also gives us a good insight into their background.

According to Potts, the leader of the coven was Elizabeth Southernes, better known as 'Old Mother Demdike', who had been a witch for over fifty years. Potts calls her "a sinke of villainie and mischiefe" and later "a damnable and malicious witch". Mother Demdike lived at the Malkin Tower in the forest of Pendle, which Potts describes as a "vaste place fit for her profession". (The exact position of Malkin Tower, a half-tumbled-down barn, is not known for sure, but Newchurch, Fence and Blacko are considered to have been the possible area in which it stood and where most of the leading witches met.)

On 2nd April 1612, Roger Nowell of Read, Justice of the Peace, examined certain witnesses at Fence, including Old Demdike and Old Chattox. Demdike readily confessed to the Devil's often having appeared to her in the form of a brown dog and that she had cursed the miller at Wheethead, Richard Baldwyn, because he refused to give her money, that she was possessed of a Devil called Tibb to which she had sold her soul, and that she had made images in clay of persons who she wished to harm, including Baldwyn's daughter, who had died suddenly and in what, under the circumstances, appeared to be mysterious conditions.

As a result of these and other confessions, Roger Nowell committed her for trial at Lancaster, together with her grand-daughter Alison Device, Anne Whittle, known as 'Old Chattox', and her daughter Anne Redfern. Not long after they had been committed for trial, reports reached Nowell that many witches had met on the following Good Friday at Malkin Tower and had plotted together to blow up Lancaster Castle. As a result, eight more persons were arrested and sent for trial: Elizabeth Device, daughter of Old Demdike; John Device, son of Elizabeth and brother of Alison; Alice Nutter of Roughlee Hall; Katherine Hewit and Alice Gray, both of Colne; Jane Bulcock and her son John, and Margaret Pearson of Padiham.

Old Demdike died in the Well Tower of Lancaster Castle before she could be brought to trial, but all the others were condemned by their own confession, with the exception of Alice Nutter, who maintained her innocence to the end.

Alice Nutter was quite different from the other alleged witches. She was a rich woman, with a good estate and children who were said to be of 'great hope'. Her family gave no evidence at her trial, and she refused to admit to any crime. She confessed to having gone to Malkin Tower on that fateful Good Friday, because she was a Roman Catholic and had in fact gone to Mass nearby, although to give away her secret would have meant punishment for her fellow Catholics. Many theories surround the reason for Alice Nutter's arrest, because there is no doubt that she was in no way connected with the others. Perhaps there was jealousy because she considered herself superior to her neighbours; perhaps, as some people suggest, she was the victim of the spite of Nowell himself, because there is evidence to suggest that he was beaten by the Nutter family in a lawsuit. Whatever the reason, evidence was given by Jennet Device, another grand-daughter of Old Demdike, that Alice Nutter had been one of the witches at the famous meeting at Malkin Tower. However, since Alice protested her innocence, the judge arranged for the calling of an identity parade – probably one of the earliest recorded. Each time the parade was held, Jennet identified Alice as the one seen at Malkin Tower, and it was mainly as a result of this that Alice Nutter was condemned.

After the trials, Jennet Device was described as being a "young infant, raised up through the wonderful work of God", because she helped to bring the witches to justice. Evidently Potts and others who made this and similar statements did not know Jennet as well as they should, for in reality she seems to have had no love for her family or neighbours, and even at the tender age of nine years she was only too ready to damn her grandmother, mother, brother and sister with her evidence. It is ironical to note that she herself was brought to trial for witchcraft in 1633.

During August 1612, a total of nineteen people were tried, including the twelve mentioned. Of these, nine were found 'not guilty'; Demdike had of course, died in prison; Margaret Pearson was sentenced to stand in the pillory at Lancaster, Clitheroe, Whalley and Padiham and was also sentenced to one year's imprisonment. The others, as have been seen, were all hanged on Thursday, 20th August 1612, less than twenty-four hours after being sentenced.

The second group of witches stood trial in 1633 after a boy named Edmund Robinson, of Wheatley Lane, told the local Justices of the Peace a long-drawn-out story about the goings on at a local witches' coven, which he claimed to have witnessed.

He said he had put two dogs on a leash and that one of them turned into a witch, while the other turned into a horse, which bore him away to a witches' coven at Hoarstones (now called 'Fence'). There he claimed to have seen six people pulling on hanging-ropes from which they obtained smoking flesh, butter and milk. He also said he had watched them making clay images. He claimed to have had many other adventures both wonderful and curious, which he related in great detail. As a result of these testimonies, Edmund found notoriety as a witch-finder, and his father took him around neighbouring churches, where the young lad seems to have had a lovely time of it, denouncing many members of the congregations as witches. As a result nineteen or twenty people were hauled off to Lancaster and tried for witchcraft. Later the boy confessed that the stories he had told were untrue, but by that time the harm had been done.

The names of all the accused are not now known, but we do know that many were relatives of the 1612 witches, including Jennet Device. At the trial seventeen persons were found guilty, but sentence was postponed until after they had been examined by the Bishop of Chester, who ordered that four of them be sent to London to be examined by the King's physicians and by the King himself.

It was reported on 15th June 1634 that three of the unfortunates had died in prison while in London, and that the fourth, Margaret Johnson, had confessed to being a witch, saying that she had sold her soul to a man who was dressed in black and whom she met in Marsden (now Nelson).

Another woman who was examined as a result of Edmund Robinson's witch findings was twenty-year-old Mary Spencer of Burnley. She denied the charges, stating that both her father and mother had both been condemned for witchcraft and had both died in prison. She said that on Sundays she usually went to Burnley Church and, at the request of the Bishop of Chester, repeated the Creed and the Lord's Prayer.

The wife of one John Dickinson of Pendle was also among those examined. She denied that she was a witch and maintained that Edmund had told lies about her, because her husband had refused to help the boy's father. Two well-known men, John Hargreaves of Higham and John Radcliffe of Heyhouses, made impassioned pleas on the poor girl's behalf.

Of course there were other areas of Lancashire where alleged witches were brought to trial. Many never got into print but passed into folk-lore and were spoken about in front of the fire on cold winters' nights. In the mid-seventeenth century the name of Sybil Farclough had only to be whispered to strike terror into the hearts of the good souls of Orrell, for she was alleged to have murdered several people, and her powers of witchcraft, coupled with a malicious and wicked tongue, held people in constant fear of their lives. She was said to have caused the deaths by witchcraft of Anne Corliss and John Naylor at some time between 1634 and 1638.

One Jane Chisnall of Little Bolton complained to the magistrates in July 1634 that her mother had been killed by witchcraft and that her brother and sister had been afflicted by a mysterious illness. She alleged that her brother had, at some time in the recent past, called the mother of one Richard Nuttall a witch. Nuttall warned him to be careful what he said, "for my mother will take courses with thee." The following day Jane's brother had fallen ill, suffering extreme pain, and the family had been forced to call on Mother Nuttall to ask if she

Hall 'i th'Wood, Bolton, haunted by the ghost of a Cavalier,
thought to be a member of the Brownlow family.

Samlesbury churchyard, in which can be found a grave with iron spikes driven through it, supposedly to stop a witch from getting out.

would visit him and remove the spell.

Mother Nuttall offered to pray for the lad, and indeed he soon got better, but not long afterwards their mother fell very ill and within a few weeks was dead, caused, said Jane Chisnall, by Mother Nuttall's transferring the spell from her brother.

The 'magician' John Dee (already mentioned in connection with Kempnough Hall, Worsley) was born in London of Welsh parentage, in 1527. During the reign of Mary Tudor (1553–8), rumours of his devilish practices caused the Queen to suspect him of endangering her life by his enchantments, but he was acquitted of the charge and went on to serve at the Court of Elizabeth, who was fascinated by his astrological predictions and his experiments in necromancy. Although he held a sinister reputation, he was a respected figure at Court, to the extent that it was he who was asked to predict an astrologically suitable date upon which to fix her coronation in 1558.

Dee met and became partners with Edward Kelly, an old Oxford scholar, who had fallen foul of the law on several occasions and wore a black cap which he pulled well down, after his ears had been cut off for some serious offence at Lancaster. For over eight years these two men were to terrify people with their dabblings into the occult.

In 1583 the gruesome twosome fled to Bohemia after narrowly escaping with their lives, when an angry mob burst into Dee's house, destroying his precious collection of books. In Bohemia they increased their reputation for invoking spirits, but by then John Dee was becoming disillusioned with the avaricious Kelly. In the end they had a serious argument, and Dee returned to England, where he accepted Elizabeth's appointment to the Wardenship of Chetham's Hospital, Manchester, a post he held for six or seven years, continuing with his experiments into the black arts and receiving numerous visits from notable members of some of Lancashire's most respected families. However, he was feared as a master of the black arts, and eventually he was forced, through his unsavoury reputation, to move out of Manchester to Mortlake, where, after years of unpopularity, he died in 1608.

Kelly, meantime, had entered into an unholy alliance with one Paul Waring, who was himself dedicated to the pursuit of wealth. Hearing that a citizen of Walton-le-Dale had recently died leaving an undiscovered fortune, Kelly and Waring went to St Leonard's churchyard where they located the new grave and by necromancy induced the corpse to rise and divulge the secret of the hidden wealth. During this midnight session, other predictions were said to have been made by the corpse, which afterwards proved remarkably accurate. Later Kelly went to Germany where he was knighted and for a time enjoyed enormous popularity, but eventually he was imprisoned for a further serious offence. Kelly died in 1595, through injuries received while trying to escape through a window.

On the road from Longridge to Whittingham, just up Halfpenny Lane, stands a charming old house, built in 1616, known as 'Old Rib House', which is associated with a Longridge witch.

Two or three centuries ago, there was a long, hot drought, and the local farmers and villagers found themselves fighting for survival. The wells dried up; fields turned brown, and the local people and their animals grew steadily more listless and thin through a combination of heat and hunger.

A kindly farmer had a dun cow of giant proportions, and to help the villagers, he allowed her to wander so that anyone in need could help themselves to her milk. The grateful villagers drew upon the plentiful supply of milk until one morning an old hag, reputed to be a witch, rose early and beat them all to it. With a cackle she seated herself beside the dun cow and gleefully proceeded to milk it into a sieve until the generous beast collapsed of exhaustion and died in front of the angry villagers.

They mourned the loss of the cow deeply and preserved her massive skeleton for many years, a rib being mounted over the lintel of the old house up Halfpenny Lane, in memory. As so often happens in this type of story, a practical-joker was once said to have removed the rib and thrown it into Charnley Brook, but so much bad luck followed that he was only too pleased to retrieve it and return it to its rightful place over the lintel at Old Rib House, where I last saw it, still in the same position, in 1974.

To most of us, witchcraft may seem rather weird and fictitious, but the memory of the Lancashire witches lingers still, particularly in the areas around Pendle and, to a lesser extent, the Fylde. On fine summer Sundays, hordes of tourists visit Alice Nutter's old home, Roughlee Hall, now converted into four separate private dwellings, and the grave of the witch in St Mary's churchyard, Newchurch-in-Pendle – the very graveyard where, according to evidence at her trial, Old Demdike had been stealing teeth from the skulls of the dead to use in magic charms.

Whalley Church has a pew which once belonged to Roger Nowell, and one can still see the marks on the font where locks were fitted to hold down a cover which was said to prevent the witches from stealing Holy Water to use in their secret ceremonies.

Lancashire is witch-country, an area of vast, uninhabited moors, crossed only in places by a few paths and with only a few small villages. There are no witches there today, brewing up magic potions, casting spells on the unwary or milking the cows dry. At least, no one will admit to there being any.

16

GHOSTLY ANIMALS, HELL HOUNDS AND RABBITS

Less pleasant than some of the phantoms one might meet in the houses of Lancashire are the strange beasts that roam by night in many parts of the county, sometimes foretelling the death of the person they meet. It was a creature such as this that inspired Sir Arthur Conan Doyle to write *The Hound of the Baskervilles*.

Tales concerning these creatures are told all over Lancashire, at Clitheroe, Droylsden, Singleton-on-the-Fylde, Ratcliffe Tower, Levens Hall, Bispham Hall etc. At Wier, locals talk of guardian hounds which protect them and lead them over the moors at night, although most are of the other, more malevolent type, like the black dog that haunted the Old Hall at Clitheroe, known as 'Old Trash', who is said to have walked Lowergate and Wellgate to Wells House.

These beasts are not exclusively British either: similar 'Hell Hounds' abound in Europe and are linked either with the stories that date back to the dogs of pagan Nature gods or with the old Norse mythology of the 'Wolf of Hell', who is said to symbolize the death that springs from sin. Be that as it may, the thought of such beasts used to terrify our ancestors.

In 1825, a man named Drabble claimed to have been attacked by an immense headless black dog, near Manchester Old Church. To his horror, he said, the creature followed him all the way home, with its front paws resting on his shoulders!

Formby foreshore, near Southport, is reputed to be the haunt of a giant black, ghostly hound with luminous eyes, the sight of which is said to bring death or severe misfortune to the beholder. Neston has a similar spectre, with a similar legend behind it.

One of the best known of these 'Hell Hounds' is a black shaggy dog, with spreading feet and drooping ears, which was said to haunt the area around Burnley Parish Church for many years and also Godley Lane. He was known as 'Old Skryker' or 'Trash', from the noise he made while walking, 'like old shoes on a miry road'. He shrieked at all times and was said to be about the width of a lane and the size of a woolsack; flames came from his mouth, and his eyes were as big as dinner-plates. Although it might be seen, the hound could not be struck because it had no substance. If anyone followed, it retreated backwards keeping its eyes fixed on its pursuer and vanishing when their attention wandered for a second or two. He would have been quite a sight, particularly after a few drinks in 'The Sparrow Hawke' across the road.

One of his more playful habits was to perch on a fence or gate-post, ready to pounce on the shoulders of some unsuspecting passer-by. However, if a Yorkshireman approached, he was said to shriek in terror and vanish with a loud splashing noise!

The Hurstwood area of Burnley was also reputed to have been plagued by a black dog, which sometimes took the form of a rag of white linen, vanishing in a flash whenever anyone tried to grasp it. It was both spiteful and mischievous, but it was eventually laid to rest near Hoggarths Cross, promising never to trouble man again, as long as a drop of water runs through Holden Clough – a promise he appears to have kept, so far.

Of course, ghostly dogs are recorded, even today. One was seen in 1957.

Paddy, as he became known, is a small black phantom dog seen in the garden of an old house at the junction of Spath Road and Holme Road in the Didsbury district of Manchester. He was seen on a clear, moonlit night by a Manchester policeman, walking across the lawn and vanishing behind a large tree. When the policeman looked behind the tree, the dog was nowhere to be seen. Intrigued, the young constable decided to investigate the mystery in broad daylight. He was surprised to find in the garden, where the dog had suddenly vanished, a small moss-covered stone at the base of the tree. On it, he read the inscription, "Paddy. Died 2nd September 1913."

Mrs Fowler, who now lives in retirement in Canada, had an interesting experience with a ghostly dog, early in this century, at her childhood home in Wigan. She came from a large family of eight girls and four boys, and, understandably, the family was quite poor. Because of the size of the family, the eight girls slept in one large bed, 'top to tail'.

One night, when all the girls were in bed, they heard the soft padding of footsteps on the stairs and were surprised when a large black dog came into the room. One of the younger girls got out of bed and went as if to stroke the dog, but her sisters cautioned her that it might bite. With that, the child climbed back into bed, and the dog went underneath it. From under the bed, they could hear the dog crunching what sounded to be a bone. The eldest of the sisters shouted down to her father, to ask whether or not he had brought a dog home. Father replied that he had not and told the girls to go to sleep.

This visitation happened quite frequently, and in the end the girls became used to the dog's coming into the room, going under the bed and crunching what sounded like a bone. Each morning when they got up, there was never a trace of either dog or bone. The girls were never able to solve the mystery while they lived at the house.

A couple of years passed, and the family fortunes improved, resulting in a move to a bigger house. The new occupants were then a young couple with a small boy. Several months after they moved in, the dog again appeared in the bedroom, which was now occupied by the boy, who, on seeing it, got out of bed to pet the animal. The dog attacked him and left him in such a terrible condition that he had to spend a long time in hospital.

Subsequent enquiries revealed that a tenant who had lived in the house about fifty years before these events took place, had been a miserly old man, who had no friends and who did not wish to become involved with the neighbours. To enable him to retain some privacy, he had bought himself a big black dog, renowned through the area for its ferocity. The old man had slept in this room, and each night his guard dog would come upstairs with him and sit by his bed until the old man gave him a bone. The dog would then disappear with the bone under the bed, where he stayed until the following morning.

Far fetched? Well, a similar incident has been recorded by the Ainsworth family who lived at Smithills Hall, Bolton, not so many years ago.

At Smithills Hall there was a room which was for many years preserved as it had been in the days of George Marsh and which was known as 'The Dead Room', due to the fact that, when members of the family died, they were laid out in this room, prior to burial. This and other rooms on this passage were reputed to be haunted by a cat, and they were used as spare bedrooms only in cases of emergency.

One day several cousins of the Ainsworths were kidding each other about the ghostly cat, and, for a dare, some of them agreed to sleep in the haunted wing. The following morning at breakfast it was noticed that they had long scratches on their faces, which no one could account for; they spoke with caution on the subject of the phantom cat after this!

It is not only dogs and cats which haunt the county: horses and even rabbits are spoken of in folk-tales. Rochdale has a ghostly bunny, known locally as 'the Baum Rabbit', whose legend goes back to the middle of the eighteenth century, when St Mary's Church was founded and the graveyard opened. The churchyard soon became known as 'the Baum', which is derived from an old Lancashire term for a herb which grew there and was used throughout the area to cure anything from bed-wetting to boils.

Years ago, a ghostly rabbit used to revisit the churchyard. It was a healthy-looking animal, lively and plump enough to last a family for two meals, which suggested that churchyard herbs agreed with it. The rabbit was said to be whiter than driven snow, always beautiful and clean, and to have always been seen rummaging among the churchyard rubbish as if in search of hidden treasure, although no one was able to get very close to it, for the slightest sound or movement is said to have caused it to disappear into thin air.

Tradition has it that, many years ago, some foul deed was perpetrated on this spot, and as a result the rabbit was doomed to haunt the area. It is on record as having frightened many local residents but has not been seen, so far as I can ascertain, within living memory, though the story is kept alive today by the local children who can often be heard reciting the following poem:

Confound that rabbit!
I wish someone would grab it,
To stop its nightly habit.
Confound that Baum rabbit.

Confound its head and eyes!
Confound its legs and thighs!
Confound it otherwise!
Confound that Baum rabbit.

Dogs rush out and squeeze him!
Worry him and tease him!
That's if you can seize him.
Confound that Baum rabbit.

In the late-nineteenth century, the villagers around Crank and Rainford, near St Helens, lived in fear of spotting 'the White Rabbit of Crank', a ghostly bunny described as being large and with 'lopping great ears', who was said to jump out at travellers and hop alongside them. Several people are said to have died in mysterious circumstances after encountering it, and those who lived to tell of their experiences knew that the sighting was an indication of approaching trouble. After the building of the railway line to Rainford Junction, it appears that the trains scared the ghostly rodent away.

The legend which accounts for the white rabbit goes back to the days of James I, a superstitious man who had a deep-rooted fear of witchcraft, as we have seen. In that credulous age of the Stuarts it is not in the least surprising that a man such as Matthew Hopkins should come along and style himself 'Witchfinder General'.

Round about this time, an old woman of foreign extraction lived a solitary existence with her grand-daughter, Jenny, in the tiny village of Crank. The old woman was held in awe by the villagers, mainly because of her knowledge of herbal remedies and their powers of healing, and, since she was thought to have studied the black arts, was reputed to be a witch.

There also lived in the area at that time a man by the name of Pullen, a repulsive character, single and miserly, who was found to be suffering from a wasting disease and resorted to obtaining some herbal remedy from Jenny's old grannie. Despite this, or because of it, his health continued to decline, and he was convinced that the old crone was trying to poison him.

He determined to break the spell the old woman had over him by resorting to a method recognized as the only way of obtaining relief in such circumstances, that of drawing blood from the witch. To help him, he enlisted the help of a worthless character called Dick Piers, the local poacher, who had been thrown out of the army because of his bad character, an unusual thing in those days. Together, their faces blackened and disguised, they set out one dark night for the old woman's cottage.

They burst in on the sleeping old woman, dragged her out of bed and made a cut on her arm, causing the blood to flow. Young Jenny, hearing her cries, rushed into the room, carrying her pet rabbit in her arms. Seeing the two men and her grandmother in a state of agitation, the frightened girl ran down the stairs and out into the black night. Pullen and Piers gave chase and saw her disappear over the crest of a hill, heading towards Billinge Beacon. When they approached the top, Jenny's rabbit hopped out of the hedge and confronted them. Swearing, Piers kicked the poor creature up into the air, and they both continued kicking the lifeless body when it landed on the ground nearby. However, they could find no trace of Jenny.

Next day, a farmer found the body of the little girl, cold and stiff, her feet torn and her head cut where she had fallen. Her grandmother soon recovered from her ordeal, and after poor Jenny's funeral, she moved out of her cottage to a more friendly environment.

The whole affair would have been forgotten had it not been for the white rabbit. Dick Piers was making his way home one day when, to his horror, he saw, hopping across the fields towards him, Jenny's rabbit. There was no mistaking the animal: there was not another like it, with its enormous white ears and great pink eyes. Terrified, Piers ran home as fast as he could, but it was too late, he was a doomed man. The white rabbit began to haunt his imagination, and the crime soon began to weigh on his mind. After a few weeks he could take no more and decided to make a full confession of his share in the crime. Then, one morning, he was found at the bottom of the local quarry, apparently having committed suicide.

Pullen, however, had no such conscience, and he lived on, becoming more sullen and morose and his health continuing to decline. Then one night, he too happened to pass the old woman's deserted cottage, when, looking down, he saw that a large white rabbit was keeping him company. He too recognized the animal and, gripped with fear, suddenly lost all his bravado and ran. The rabbit ran too. He turned, and the rabbit also turned. He stopped, and the rabbit stopped. In sheer desperation he ran like the wind across the fields to his home finally collapsing with sheer exhaustion within sight of the lights of his house. He was found several hours later, suffering from fright and exposure, and within a week he too was dead.

People insist that 'the White Rabbit of Crank' is still seen on dark nights, and those that see it can be assured of ill-fortune ahead. A few years ago, when I lived near Crank and had to travel from Liverpool every day, I used to come off the East Lancashire Road at Windle and travel through Crank to Billinge. During the winter months it was quite eerie on those quiet roads, and had I known about the white rabbit in those days, then perhaps I might have pushed my luck and stayed on the East Lancashire Road, despite all its hazards.

Ghostly horses are also quite popular in the county. Bourn Hall near Fleetwood was supposed to have a ghostly horse, wild-looking and with fetlocks steaming, which roamed the surrounding farm-lands on wild moonlit nights. Not far away, at Hackensall Hall, just across the River Wyre from Fleetwood, they were once said to be plagued by a boggart horse who remained helpful and inoffensive just so long as they kept a fire going all night in the kitchen, where he could bed down after ploughing the fields when it became dark. During some alterations to the Hall some years ago, two skeletons, thought to be female, were discovered bricked up in the walls. No one knows much about them, but the phantom horse has been linked with them.

A ghostly horse haunted the Round House at Blundellsands in the late-eighteenth century – the time when it became fashionable to bathe in the sea for health reasons, and when the Round House was a bathing-lodge, with a horse stabled there to pull the bathing-machines into the water, at a discreet depth, before the naked bather ventured out into the water. Some years ago the property underwent extensive alterations and during that time the owners noticed some rather strong, and at times embarrassing, stable smells and the sound of a restless horse stamping in its stall. As the alterations progressed, a large bone from a horse's foreleg was unearthed. Later, when it had been quietly re-buried, the manifestations ceased.

Various other furry and feathered ghosts have aroused fear in the area from time to time. A family at Whitworth was often visited by a ghostly shadowy bird resembling a crow or raven, whose appearance, which was accompanied by a pecking sensation, usually heralded a death in the family. At Hambledon there were a couple of ghostly cats, one haunting Sower Carr Lane, the other, described as a giant, friendly old moggie, rubbing against the legs of wayfarers as a pet cat would do when seeking human companionship. A boggart cat was also reported at Preesall – a most unusual and military pussycat, dressed in a lovely scarlet tunic, said to haunt a lane which has long since disappeared and which led to some old cottages at Town Foot.

Was it really the barking of a fox or the cry of a wild goose you heard the other night? Or was it one of Lancashire's night animals, which, as the moon rides across the night sky, seek the shadows where we mere mortals dare not venture?

17

LANCASHIRE WELLS

There are many wells familiar to Lancashire folk, around which legends have been written, and just over the border at Giggleswick there is the Ebbing and Flowing Well which has a history going back to prehistoric times.

St Oswald's Well, at Winwick, is said to be the spot where the martyr bled to death, the blood-soaked earth bringing about sensational cures for all kinds of diseases and infirmity: so much of this blood-stained earth was taken away by pilgrims that water began to seep into the hole and was soon taken up by the local Catholic churches, to be used as Holy Water. The well of St Marie, at Blackburn, possessed powers of healing, as did the fresh clear spring known as 'Walloper Well' up on Waddington Fells. But of all the wells in the county, St Anne's Well and Peg O'Nell's Well have, in my opinion, the more fascinating legends attached to them.

A mile or so south of St Helens town centre is Sherdley Park. For many years a small priory had stood not far to the south-west of here which has long since disappeared, but I believe that at one time its site was marked by an old farmhouse, built on the foundations. It had an extensive estate stretching on every side and was run by a shrewd and good-hearted Prior, Father Delwaney.

Every monastery had its patron saint, its images and relics, and Sutton Priory had for its patron St Anne. Among its 'furniture', the most valuable was a well named after her, situated about half a mile from where Rainhill railway station now stands, very near the boundary which divided the Priory lands from those of Sir Richard Bold, who owned great portions of the lands in Sutton and Rainhill.

The well had a reputation throughout the area for the medicinal properties its waters possessed, the cure of skin diseases being its speciality. It was said that the curative powers had been conferred on the well by St Anne herself, who at some time or other had bathed in its waters.

For two or three years, considerable ill-feeling had existed between Father Delwaney and Hugh Darcy, steward of Sir Thomas Bold, the neighbouring landowner, owing to a dispute between them as to rights of access to the well and the position of the boundaries between certain parts of the estates. Darcy was a bully who looked after no interest but his own and was capable of going to great lengths against anyone who stood in his way. After one argument with the Prior, he threatened to summon the King's Commissioners and have the Priory closed. Father Delwaney was alarmed at this, being well aware of the perilous uncertainty the monasteries were in at that time.

A couple of days later, Darcy arrived at Sutton Priory accompanied by the King's Commissioners, who presented to the Prior the Vicar General's order for their removal from the Priory and showed orders to take possession of it in the name of the King. Darcy could not refrain from sneering at the position in which the monks found themselves. Seeing this, the angry Father Delwaney spat at him: "The curse of the serpent be upon thee, thou spoiler of the Lord's inheritance. Thy ill-gotten gains shall not profit thee, and a year and a day shall not pass ere St Anne thy head shall bruise."

Darcy turned pale, cowed by the Prior's fixed gaze, and, coward that he was, struck the now restrained Prior. Turning on his heels, with a contemptuous laugh he strode away. Father Delwaney died soon afterwards and was buried at nearby Parr Abbey, but his words haunted Darcy for weeks.

Three months after the Prior's death, Darcy's only son died from a mysterious illness, then Darcy himself began to decline. Having lost heavily on gambling and lost his job as steward to Sir Thomas Bold through drunkenness, nothing could stop the downward career of the bully, who went from bad to worse.

One night he got drunk at an inn near Micklehead, and it was late before he left to return home to Rainhill. He never made it. At daybreak, his wife, who had waited up all night for his return with the greatest anxiety, aroused the neighbours and asked them to help her search for him. The shortest route home from the inn was along the footpath past St Anne's Well, and it was here the search began. When they reached the well, they found Darcy dead at the bottom of the well with his head crushed in. Such was his end: the Prior's prediction had now been fulfilled.

The other well is at Bungerley Bridge, to the north-west of Clitheroe, which was once part of the Lancashire-Yorkshire border and replaced the former Hipping Stones across the River Ribble. It was here that a well-documented incident occurred during the Wars of the Roses.

In 1463 Henry VI had been defeated at Hexham by the superior Yorkist forces and, having escaped, found sanctuary for a while with Sir Ralph Pudsey at his manor at Bolton-by-Bowland. Henry, convinced that Yorkist spies had discovered his whereabouts, quickly fled the manor and sought refuge with Sir John Tempest at Waddington Hall. But Thomas Talbot, Sir John's son-in-law, betrayed the King, and although Henry managed to escape on this occasion, he did not travel very far before being captured by Thomas Talbot and his cousin John Talbot at Bungerley Bridge. Here Henry was bound to the stirrups of his horse and taken a prisoner to London.

Should one visit Bungerley Bridge, as I did, on a warm summer weekend, this beautiful spot will be swarming with picnickers and the odd angler or two. But come here after a long period of rain, and the raging waters will invoke a reminder of Peg O'Nell whose ghost haunts this section of the River Ribble, and who appears from the murky brown water after a storm. She screams from the river on dark cold nights, and every seven years she claims a human victim, drowned in this stretch of water.

According to legend, Peg was a servant-girl employed at Waddow Hall. One day her mistress, a reputed witch, sent the girl to draw water from the well a little way down-river from the hall, cursing her as she did so, that she might slip and break her neck. The old witch must have been on form, for by all accounts the spell worked. Poor Peg slipped and fell into the turbulent river and was drowned. A number of drownings over the years have led to the superstition that Peg claimed her revenge in this way every seven years.

Several families have lived at Waddow Hall in its long history, and one family, the Starkies, were there when Peg's ghost was at its most malevolent. There was at that time a statue near Peg's Well (one of many memorials to the supplanted Catholic religion in the area), which they called 'Peg' after their ghost. The Starkies regarded this statue with distaste, and they thought themselves quite justified in ascribing to it all the mischief and evils that befell them: if a storm damaged the house, Peg, the statue, was responsible. One day, when Mr Starkie returned home late, with a broken leg, although he had been hunting all day and had afterwards made too free with the local ale, as usual Peg was blamed for his misfortune: she was said to have waylaid him and caused his horse to fall.

Before the bridge at Bungerley was built (during the early part of the nineteenth century), all travellers were compelled to cross the Ribble at this point by the old 'Hipping Stones'. One day, a clergyman was attempting to cross when the swollen, fast-running river caught him off guard, causing him to slip. Starkie was nearby and, hearing his cries, was just in time to rescue him and help the wet and uncomfortable guest to Waddow Hall. Mistress Starkie, on seeing her husband enter the Hall, panting under the huge weight of the dripping parson, went into hysterics, cursing and blaming Peg O'Nell. She rushed from the room into the garden where the statue stood and, with one blow from an axe, severed the head from the body.

The headless statue still stands near the Hall, I believe, but who she really is and who brought her here can only be speculation on my part. It is possibly a statue of St Margaret, most probably it was brought from Sawley Abbey during the Reformation, and possibly damaged during the violent days of the introduction of Protestantism, in the reign of Edward VI. Whoever it is and wherever the statue came from, for a great number of years this figure was associated with any evil happenings that took place in the vicinity.

The Hall itself is reputed to be haunted. In one room the atmosphere is said to be very cold all the year round; dogs refuse to enter, and several times a spectral mist has appeared. Some people think that the decapitated head of the statue was hidden in this room, while others say that this was the room where the unfortunate Peg slept and where she was brought on the day she died.

Peg's ghost is said to be forever seeking revenge on anyone related to her employers or, indeed, resembling them, and on animals which are their property. By her sudden appearances she frightens both humans and animals into treacherous pools of the river, where they are drowned. It has even been suggested that some of these animals may have been sacrificed, for the belief is that Peg O'Nell's spirit can be appeased only if a small bird or animal is held under the stretch of water she haunts, until the poor creature has drowned.

18

LANCASHIRE KNIGHTS

There used to be a comic postcard sold on Blackpool promenade which showed a bleary-eyed knight. The caption underneath said, "Once a king, always a king, but once a knight is enough." If one considers the sort of adventures some of the Lancashire knights are said to have had, then this caption would have been nearer the truth than the saucy postcard's designer had imagined.

One of the most famous of all the knights of old was, of course, Sir Lancelot, and his story starts in the township of Holmeswood, which lies between Formby and Ormskirk on part of what is believed to have been the largest inland lake in the country, Lake Linius or Martin Mere, now dry and well-cultivated but said to be still haunted by the ghosts of King Arthur's Court. One of the earliest-recorded Lancashire legends set around here concerns Sir Lancelot.

The name 'Lancelot' derives from the Celtic and literally translated means 'People's Spear'. Some historians in this part of the world argue that the word 'Lancashire' takes its name from 'Lancelot's Shire'.

He was the son of a Breton king from Benoit, who, fleeing from France, died soon after reaching England. How he died, we do not know, but he must have died somewhere beside Martin Mere, for, according to legend, his wife, Queen Helen, left her baby son beside the lake, while she attempted to save the King's life. The child was 'found' by the mistress of Merlin, the nymph Vivien, who, seeing the approach of the distraught Queen, vanished into the lake, taking the baby with her. When he was about eighteen years old, young Lancelot was taken to Camelot and presented at the Court of King Arthur, where he was knighted, becoming 'Sir Lancelot of the Lake'.

At this period of time, the Knights of the Round Table regularly sallied forth to do battle with the Saxons, and it was during one of those forays that Sir Lancelot first heard of the treacherous and cruel

St Mary's churchyard, Newchurch-in-Pendle, where Mother Demdike was allegedly seen, stealing teeth from the newly-dead to use in her magic charms.

Newchurch-in-Pendle: the grave outside St Mary's Church, said to be Alice Nutter's but marked 'Ellin Nutter', perhaps a relative.

Newchurch-in-Pendle. About the only witches to be found around Pendle today are those dummies outside a Newchurch gift-shop.

Saxon giant called Tarquin, who had a castle and lands somewhere in the Manchester area and who had many knights held prisoner in his deep dungeons. Inevitably, the gallant Sir Lancelot set out to slay Tarquin and free the knights.

On nearing the castle he met a beautiful maiden who told him he should flee and thus preserve his life, but Lancelot refused to do so and rode on, accompanied, a little way behind, by the maiden. As he approached the grim place, he saw, standing in front of the drawbridge, a tree on which hung the swords and shields of the captured knights. Also hanging from the tree was a copper basin, which visitors and gladiatorial knights must strike to summon the giant. Sir Lancelot gave the basin a mighty swipe with the flat of his sword, and soon Tarquin appeared, roaring with anger as he staggered over the drawbridge.

Sir Lancelot issued his challenge, which Tarquin took up, and the long duel began. They fought all day, the giant's sword possessing greater strength than that of the young knight. In fact, during the fight, Sir Lancelot's sword was broken, but he managed to pluck a broad sword from a branch of the tree and continued the contest. At some stage in the long-drawn-out battle, both the fighters lost their swords, and in the ensuing rush to regain a weapon, Sir Lancelot picked up Tarquin's sword and slew him.

The maiden now gave Sir Lancelot a magic horn, which she told him he must blow in order to lower the drawbridge and enable him to get to the prisoners.

Hiding inside the gateway was a dwarf, who, armed with a mace, tried to kill the good knight, but the maiden saved Lancelot's life by pushing him sharply to one side, deflecting the blow. Sir Lancelot killed the dwarf with a blow from the giant's sword and then turned to the maiden in order to thank her, but she evaporated before his eyes. He knew then that she was the nymph Vivien.

Of course, to survive as a knight in the old days, one had to be not only brave but a little crafty and determined. One such man was Sir Thomas Lathom of Lathom, who, legend says, married in 1343 and who longed for a son and heir. Unfortunately, after twelve years of marriage, his wife was unable to present him with a son, although she bore him a daughter, Isobel.

Now, being of a somewhat determined nature, Sir Thomas did not let the fact that his wife could not bear him a son stop him from looking around for someone who could. He found favour with a village girl, the lusty young daughter of a yeoman, who eventually became pregnant by him and who ultimately gave birth to a son. Now Sir Thomas, although overjoyed at the birth of a longed-for heir, had problems: how could he tell his wife that he had been unfaithful, and how would he introduce his son into his family?

In the grounds of Lathom Park was an eagle's nest, and Sir Thomas devised a plan whereby the child was left under the tree containing the nest, knowing that his wife would discover him while taking her daily walk. The following morning, as Sir Thomas and Lady Lathom walked, they 'discovered' the baby. Sir Thomas, looking suitably surprised, said that the child must have been dropped by the eagle that nested in the tree, truly a gift from heaven. The baby was taken home, and by all accounts Lady Lathom was taken in, for she accepted the story and accepted the child, having him baptized 'Oskatell'.

Later in life Oskatell served at the Court of King Edward, who knighted him 'Sir Oskatell de Lathom'. While he and his sister were at the Court at Winchester Sir John Stanley met the fair Isobel and fell instantly in love with her. He asked her father for her hand in marriage, but Sir Thomas did not consider a Stanley good enough for his daughter, so Isobel and Sir John took the only course open to them and eloped to Stafford, where they were duly married. The enraged Sir Thomas turned over his wealth to Oskatell.

However, when Sir John Stanley died, in Ireland, some years later, Isobel returned to live in Liverpool with her three children, and Sir Thomas Lathom, now an old man, was sufficiently conscience-stricken to place all his estates in his daughter's hands, leaving the manors of Irlam and Urmston to Oskatell, who was also given the crest of the eagle, his rivals, the descendants of Sir John Stanley, the present earls of Derby, taking the crest of 'the eagle and child', which they continue to hold to this day and which can be seen in many places in Lancashire, including the font at Ormskirk Church and in the shape of a plaque in a recess in the Church of All Saints at Childwell, to which it is thought to have been presented when the Stanley family became Lords of the Manor in 1473.

According to the Preston telephone-directory, there are six 'Eagle and Child' hotels or inns – how many there are in the Liverpool directory, I know not. I wonder how many people who have adopted these hostelries as their 'local', know the legend surrounding the sign over the door?

> That dragon of old who churches ate
>   (He always came on Sunday),
> To pick up fat members who came in late,
> Reserving the parson, though part of the State,
> As a tit-bit for the Monday.

This old Lancashire rhyme goes back into antiquity and recalls how the Bold family gained their estates.

In prehistoric times there existed, where the present town of Runcorn now stands, a vast forest of mighty trees. According to legend, strange animals lived in the dense undergrowth, supreme among them being a giant flying dragon who had his lair by the riverside near which Halton Castle later stood. This monster was the scourge and terror of the county for miles around: on his excursions in search of food, he always selected the best-fed sheep and cattle. Many attempts were made by the local farmers to kill the dragon, only to result in the destruction of the would-be killers themselves. The pathetic attempts, with bow and arrow, stones and slings, were looked upon with contempt by the beast. However, retributive justice was at hand, and the destruction of the dragon was affected in a way he little expected.

At Cuerdly Marsh lived a sturdy blacksmith called Robert Byrch, whose fame as a blacksmith and armourer was known throughout south Lancashire and north Cheshire. Not only was he able to shoe horses, forge spades and shape the ploughshares of his neighbours, but many a gallant knight had sought his services in the manufacture of swords and armour. Robert had seen the dragon and heard tales of its terrible deeds, and, moreover, he had heard it proclaimed in the market-place that a reward had been offered to anyone who would rid this part of the realm of the dreaded beast.

He had noticed that, so far, none of his animals that wandered near the forge had been attacked, and he thought that the dragon was probably afraid of the forge fire. However, one dull November day, just as he was hammering away with all his might at a ploughshare, the dragon swooped out of the sky and seized a cow that had been standing outside the door of the forge. Now Robert did not mind the dragon's stealing his neighbour's cattle, but when his own were being stolen before his eyes, it became a different matter. The angry blacksmith now decided that something must be done to bring this state of affairs to a halt, and he, Robert Byrch, would do it or die in the attempt.

A few days later, neighbours were surprised to see Robert leading a horse towards his forge. On its back the horse carried a load of carefully packed iron sheets of special toughness, and on top of this was the hide of a freshly killed cow, with the head and horns still attached. For several days he worked, forming a complete casing of metal into which he could creep and be protected. Jointed casings protected his arms and legs, and over all this was stretched the cow's hide with the head attached. He next made himself a short, broad, double-edged sword and fitted it with a stout buckthorn hilt, which he attached to a sheath at the side of his armour so that it could be easily reached with his right hand. Then he ordered one of his apprentices to keep a strict lookout for the monster, meanwhile practising daily in his suit of armour the movements of a grazing cow.

He did not have long to wait: on a keen frosty morning, just before Christmas, the dragon was seen leisurely flying in a circle at a distance. Without a moment's hesitation the blacksmith got into his armour, saw that his sword was in position and slowly walked out on all fours in the direction of the field. The dragon swooped down on the seemingly unsuspecting cow, and soon Robert, inside his armour, felt himself being borne into the air. Drawing his sword, he thrust it into the unprotected belly of the monster, just under the wing; a torrent of blood flowed from the wound, and the dragon began to waver in its flight. Looking down, the blacksmith saw, to his dismay, that he was immediately over the River Mersey, and he realized that if the dragon were to come down there, the weight of his armour would take him, like a stone, to the bottom. He thrust his hand into the gaping wound to stem the flow of blood until the wounded dragon finally made it to his lair. Rapidly climbing out of his armour, the brave blacksmith finished the dragon off with a mighty blow from his sword. With a feeble flap and a snort, the last icthyornis in Great Britain died on the muddy banks of the River Mersey.

News of Robert's feat reached the ears of the King, who decreed, as a reward, that the blacksmith's name should henceforth be 'Robert the Bold', in commemoration of his courage, and that as much land in the fairest part of the county as the skin of the dragon, when cut into strips, would enclose, should be granted to him and his heirs forever. The legend tells us that Sir Robert, as he had now become, cut up the dragon's skin into very fine strips and, selecting his portion of lands from the spot named after him, became the founder of the Bold family's fortune.

This is no fairy story or figment of the imagination. The aerial combat with the dragon could be seen, years ago, in graphic outlines on the wall over the kitchen fireplace at the Bold Arms Hotel at Bold Heath. For years the inhabitants of Bold and Farnworth were familiar with a skin which hung above the Bold family pew in Farnworth Church. There, high above the congregation, it hung for centuries, until in the 1870s the old relic fell to the ground. After much careful examination and the removal of the dust of centuries, it was pronounced to be the untanned hide of a cow, still bearing traces of the dragon's claws.

The Bold family, one of the oldest in the country, appear to have been of early Saxon origin, established in the area long before the Norman Conquest. The line died out in 1762 when Peter, son of Sir Richard Bold, died, leaving a daughter, Anna Maude, who, on her death in 1803, left the estates to Peter, son of Thomas Patton, husband of her sister Dorothea.

The icthyornis was some fifty feet in length, with enormous wings; his body, encased in a coat of scaly mail, was impervious to dagger or arrow, save in two places, one under each wing. Broad coloured bands or stripes decorated his enormous carcase, producing a striking resemblance to an enormous Colorado beetle, while his massive reptilian jaws, armed with rows of saw-like teeth, his huge glaring multicoloured eyes, long flexible neck and still longer flexible tail, must have made him an awesome sight.

Lastly, a dastardly deed which culminated in the death of the damsel in distress and her gallant knight errant.

Just off the A59 at Burscough, near Ormskirk, stand two pillars and a portion of wall containing one side of a window, all that remains of what was one of the most important religious houses in Lancashire, Burscough Priory.

It was founded in about 1190 for the Black Canons, an Augustinian order, and was a very rich religious house. By 1295 there was a prior and six canons, and by 1530 a prior, five monks and over forty dependants. Over the years, there have been extensive excavations which have provided us with a good idea of what the Priory was like in its heyday: there was a church with transepts, tower, chapel and chapter house, probably an almonary and almost certainly a hospital for lepers. I believe that Ormskirk Church was built from some of the stone from the Priory, and the ancient bells were also installed there. Certainly the great tenor bell, which hung in the tower, is at Ormskirk.

There is a very old and well-known legend attached to Burscough Priory, supposedly dating from the reign of Edward III, when one Michael de Pointings was sent to the Priory to seek the whereabouts of a woman named Margaret de la Beck. Who she was, and who sent Michael on the mission, I do not know. Suffice to say, he set off on his journey and, on approaching the Priory, met a strange woman who appeared to know all about his mission and who begged him to turn back. Michael refused to do as she asked. On reaching the Priory, he was taken before Prior Thomas, who denied all knowledge of the missing woman.

Michael returned to Ormskirk, where he met a man called Thomas Clarke, who told him that Margaret had been presumed drowned, although her body had not been found. Clarke went on to say that, while passing a big barn which belonged to the Priory, he had heard strange noises coming from inside it. Michael offered him some money, and Thomas Clarke agreed to show him the place.

Collecting horses and servants, Michael and Thomas Clarke set off to the barn, which was situated about a mile from the Priory. On reaching the spot, moaning could be heard, which Michael recognized as the voice of the mysterious woman he had previously met. She was dragged out and told them that her name was Isobel, admitting that she was responsible for a prisoner in one of the Priory cellars. She offered to take Michael to the place where the prisoner was held.

Isobel led the group to the dank cellar where they found poor Margaret, now completely insane after having been bound and brutally tortured. Michael picked up Margaret and was about to make good his escape when Thomas Clarke was killed by an arrow. Michael called to his servants, but it was too late, and an arrow found a vital spot, killing him instantly. The servants rode off, taking Michael's body and carrying Margaret to a safe place, where she too died soon after.

The story soon came out, but as the Prior was so much in the King's favour, he was granted a pardon for his crimes against Margaret de la Beck and the murder of Michael de Pointings and Thomas Clarke.

19

LEGENDS OF THE CHURCH

There are enough legends surrounding the Church to fill several volumes. This is understandable when one considers how the Roman Catholic Church suffered during the sixteenth century, when Lancashire perhaps held on to the Catholic Faith for longer than most other counties. Of course, not all the legends are of this period: some go back further in time than recorded history and have been passed on from one generation to the next. However, most of the following legends relate to the sixteenth century, not because the earlier ones are not worth recording but because they appeal to me personally.

According to popular legend, the tower of Whalley Church contained five bells, which at different periods were presented to various neighbouring families. Three were at Downham, and attached to these bells is the belief that, as shepherds passed over Pendle Hill on calm nights, particularly at Ashendean Clough, they could hear the soft, low chimes of distant bells – 'The Monks' Bells'. Knowing that the bells of Clitheroe, Whalley and Ribchester would be silent at this hour, they believed that the chimes came from the old bells in Downham steeple, still calling the monks to prayer at midnight.

Many people know that Catherine Parr, the last wife of Henry VIII, was born at Kendal Castle, in 1512. Not many are aware, though, that one branch of the Parr family was of Lancashire origin, coming from 'a district lying west of the Mersey', now part of St Helens.

Some members of the Parr family were connected with a monastery dedicated to St Helen and erected in Derby at the time of King Stephen, in about 1140. During the reign of Edward I there is a record of one 'Parre' associated with it, an association which possibly gave the name to the present town.

About a mile from the town centre, on the east side of the town, stands the Parr Industrial Estate, and it is in this area that Parr Hall, the home of the Parr family, once stood. In the sixteenth century, this old hall was a spacious, rambling edifice, part-farm, part-monastery and part-mansion. Besides a few cottages and a hostelry, 'The Swan', situated near the Sankey Brook, there were no other dwellings for miles.

Our story begins during the reign of Henry VIII, when a royal messenger, with orders to travel night and day, was rapidly making his way to this obscure corner of the realm. He pulled up at the shuttered and bolted inn, ordering the landlord to open up, "in the King's name". After a hasty meal, the horseman enquired of the whereabouts of Parr Hall and was soon demanding a fresh horse to carry him the remainder of his journey. Quickly mounting, he set off over the rickety wooden bridge, rotten with age and neglect, which promptly collapsed under the weight of the horse and rider, plunging them both into the dark, fast-running stream below. The landlord rescued both horse and rider, taking him back to the inn; he told the messenger that there was a monk at Parr, well-skilled in healing, and he would set out to bring him back to attend to the rider's injuries. Early the next morning, mine host, good as his word, set out for Parr Abbey. His news created a sensation at the Abbey, the visit of a royal messenger being a very rare event. Quickly the Abbot prepared to tend the man's injuries. Returning to the inn, with the landlord and a monk, the Abbot found the poor messenger in great pain. He said to the injured man: "I hear thou bearest urgent news from our royal lady, Queen Catherine." The messenger asked if he was being addressed by the Abbot of Parr and, when he learned that he was, he handed him a personal letter from the Queen herself, warning him to expect much adversity, as King Henry had remembered the Abbey at Parr and was soon to send his commissioners to suppress it.

Silently, and with heavy hearts, the Abbot and the monk rode back to the Abbey. As they neared the gates, a lay brother, leading a strange horse across the courtyard, observed their approach and, throwing down the rein, ran out to meet them. Had the King's commissioners arrived? The Abbot's heart nearly failed him and, unable to speak, he signalled the brother to unfold his news.

"The King is dead!" he cried.

"Then we are safe," exclaimed the Abbot joyfully as he rode through the gate.

That, then, is how providence lent a hand in saving Parr Abbey during the suppression of the monasteries. Throughout the reign of Edward and Mary it continued to flourish, but it soon began to decline, so that by the time of Elizabeth I it had become lost in obscurity. Under the Stuarts it was simply a large farmhouse with out-buildings. Today a more modern structure stands on the site.

Preserved in the Roman Catholic Chapel at Ashton-in-Makerfield, is a remarkable relic which people over a wide area of Lancashire and Cheshire believe to have wonderful powers of healing – the remains of the hand of Father Edmund Arrowsmith.

Father Arrowsmith was born at nearby Haydock in 1585 and was dedicated to the Roman Catholic faith. He entered the Jesuit College at Douay and, although at the time English priests were outlawed and faced certain death, he was ordained in 1612.

In 1623 Father Arrowsmith was betrayed and subsequently arrested and carted off to Lancaster to face trial. There, in the face of all the bigotry, cruelty and brow-beating of the era, he was charged with being a Roman priest, "contrary to the laws of his Majesty", and the case was proved against him. He was found guilty and sentenced to death, "as prescribed by law". Before his execution, Father Arrowsmith asked one of his friends to sever a hand, with the assurance that although he would be no longer of this world, he would still, through his lifeless hand, be able to perform miracles. In due course the hand was severed and taken to Bryn Hall, near Ashton-in-Makerfield and kept in the safe custody of the Gerrard family. Many people were convinced of the remarkable healing powers of the hand, and made long, weary journeys to receive the miraculous healing powers.

When one of the early owners of Ince Hall lay on his death bed, a lawyer was sent for at the last moment to make his Will. However, before the lawyer reached the Hall, the man was dead. The lawyer, in his dilemma, decided to try the effect of the hand on the corpse. The body of the dead man was rubbed all over with the hand, and it was said that he had revived sufficiently to sign his Will.

After the funeral, his daughter produced a second Will which was not signed, leaving the Hall to the son and daughter. The lawyer, however, soon produced his Will, signed by the dead man and conveying all the property to him. The son, rightly suspecting fraud, quarrelled with the lawyer and, after wounding him and thinking him dead, left the country and was never heard of again. The daughter also disappeared most mysteriously, no one knew how or where – until, after many years, a gardener turned up a skull in the grounds, and the secret was finally out.

When this took place, the Hall had long been uninhabited, for the murdered girl's ghost hung suspended in the air before the lawyer wherever he went. It is said that he spent his remaining years in Wigan, the victim of remorse and despair. There was a room in the Hall which was said to be haunted by the ghost of a young woman, and her shadowy form was seen quite frequently, hovering over the spot where her remains were buried.

However, back to the sacred hand. As late as the turn of the nineteenth century, implicit faith in the power of the hand was held by many, and it is recorded that in 1872 a woman, wholly destitute, walked all the way from Salford in order to have the holy hand placed upon her, one side of her body being paralysed. The Wigan Board of Guardians stated at that time that hundreds of people had visited the township for the same reason.

When Bryn Hall was demolished, the hand was removed to Garswood, until finally being placed in the Catholic Chapel at Ashton-in-Makerfield.

There is a rather eerie legend, slightly more up to date, told about Lancaster Priory, which was related to me some twenty-five or thirty years ago by the then verger.

Many years ago, when it was safe for church doors to remain unlocked, two down-and-outs found themselves in Lancaster, one cold winter's night, near the Judge's Lodgings at the foot of Castle Hill. Seeing the silhouette of the Priory nestling close to the Castle, they climbed the steep steps leading to the entrance, preferring to spend the night in the comparative comfort of the church rather than in the casual ward of the workhouse. They pushed open the heavy oak door, quietly closed it behind them and stood in the gloom of this fine historic church. Finding a warm spot towards the back, they settled down for the night.

The altar candlesticks and plate gleamed, as the moon poured through the beautiful stained-glass windows, giving them the appearance of gold. To two down-and-outs, candlesticks like these meant money, full bellies and warm beds, so perhaps they could be forgiven for their thoughts. To one of them, however, as he lay tossing in the gloom, the candlesticks took on a new meaning: they could become his passport to better things. He thought of the money they might bring and how the silver plate would set him up for the rest of his life. He would get up very early, steal the plate and candlesticks and be off before his companion awoke. He would sell them in Preston and then disappear, making a new life for himself.

Several hours later, he awoke. It was still dark. His friend was still sleeping, albeit fitfully. The man quietly rose and, glancing at his sleeping friend, stealthily made his way up the centre aisle towards the altar.

A few minutes later, the sleeping man was awakened by a terrifying scream, which seemed to emanate from the altar itself. He sat up, startled. Noticing that his friend was missing, he got up and set about to investigate, for it could only have been his companion who screamed. As he made his way towards the altar, he noticed that one of the candlesticks was missing and there, on the altar steps, lay his companion. He was dead, his face contorted in abject terror. In his hand he clutched a heavy brass candlestick.

The Black Abbey area of Accrington owes its name to a monastery of the same name, where the Black Abbots lived an almost idyllic life in what was then a most lovely area. Unfortunately, one of the brothers fell in love with a beautiful local girl, using one of the rooms in the Abbey towers as a secret meeting-place. It was only a matter of time before the girl's father found out about the affair, and one night, when the lovers were together, he burst into the room where they were. Hurriedly, the gallant monk pushed the hysterical girl into a secret passage and turned to meet the father, refusing to answer any questions about himself or the girl. Naturally, the father was, to say the least, annoyed, and he awoke the brothers of the Abbey with his shouting and swearing. The reticent monk was seized and put in chains. The monks then sealed the door and set fire to the tower.

As the helpless monk lay, waiting for the flames to reach him, he heard the voice of his sweetheart, who had now returned from the secret room into the burning tower. She tried to release him, but to no avail, and the monk begged her to escape through the secret passage and save herself. She refused and, putting her arms around him, declared that they would die together. The following morning their charred remains were found among the debris of the burned-out tower. Now, according to legend, at midnight on dark, moonless nights, the figure of the young girl can be seen emerging from the site of the Black Abbey. She is said to be dressed in a flowing white robe, her right arm withered and barren of flesh as though she had been severely burned. She is said to utter a terrifying shriek before evaporating into thin air.

INDEX